Adult Coloring book

MANDALA
Dogs & Cats

50
Stress Relieving Designs

**Copyright © 2022 – Wonderful Press
All rights reserved**

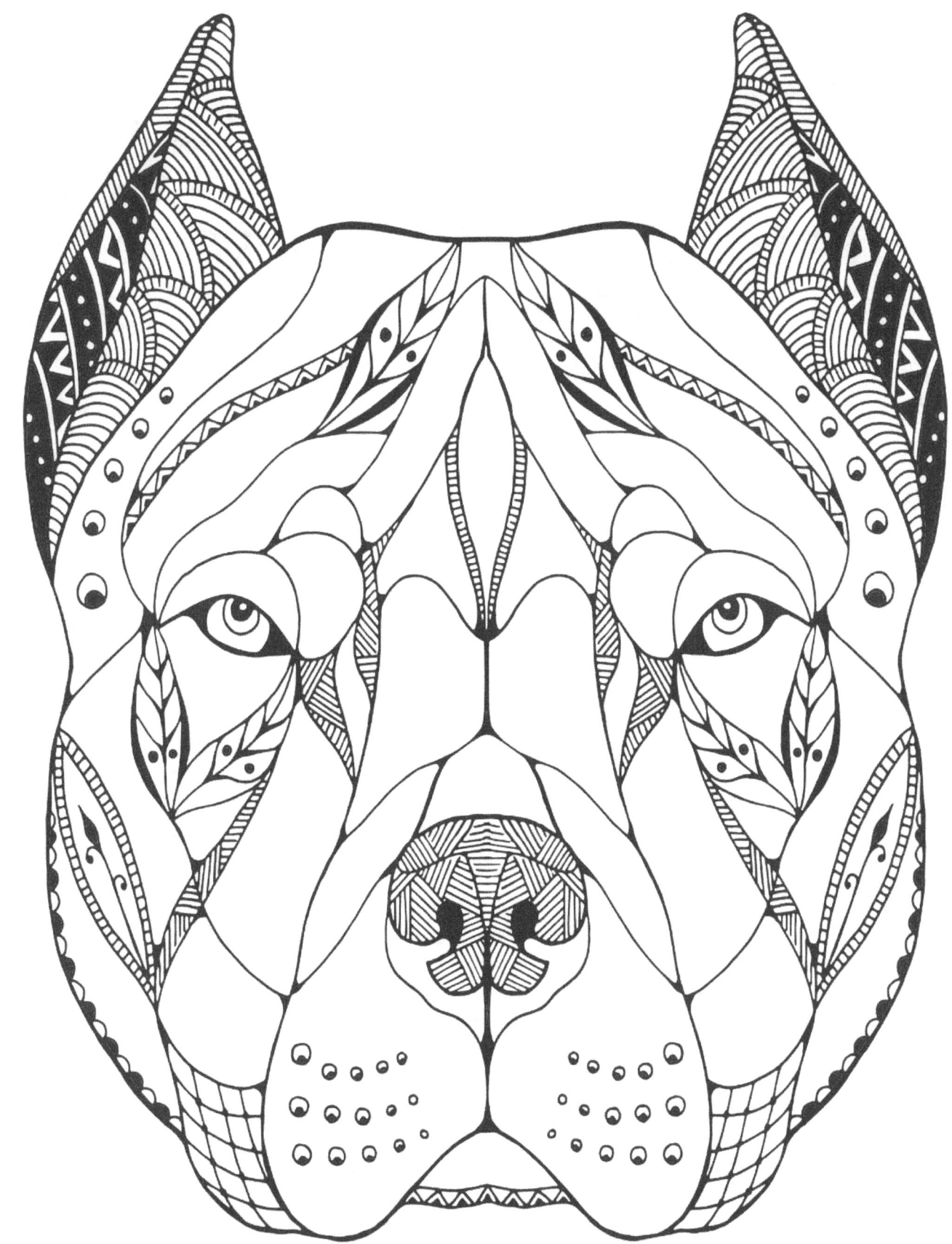

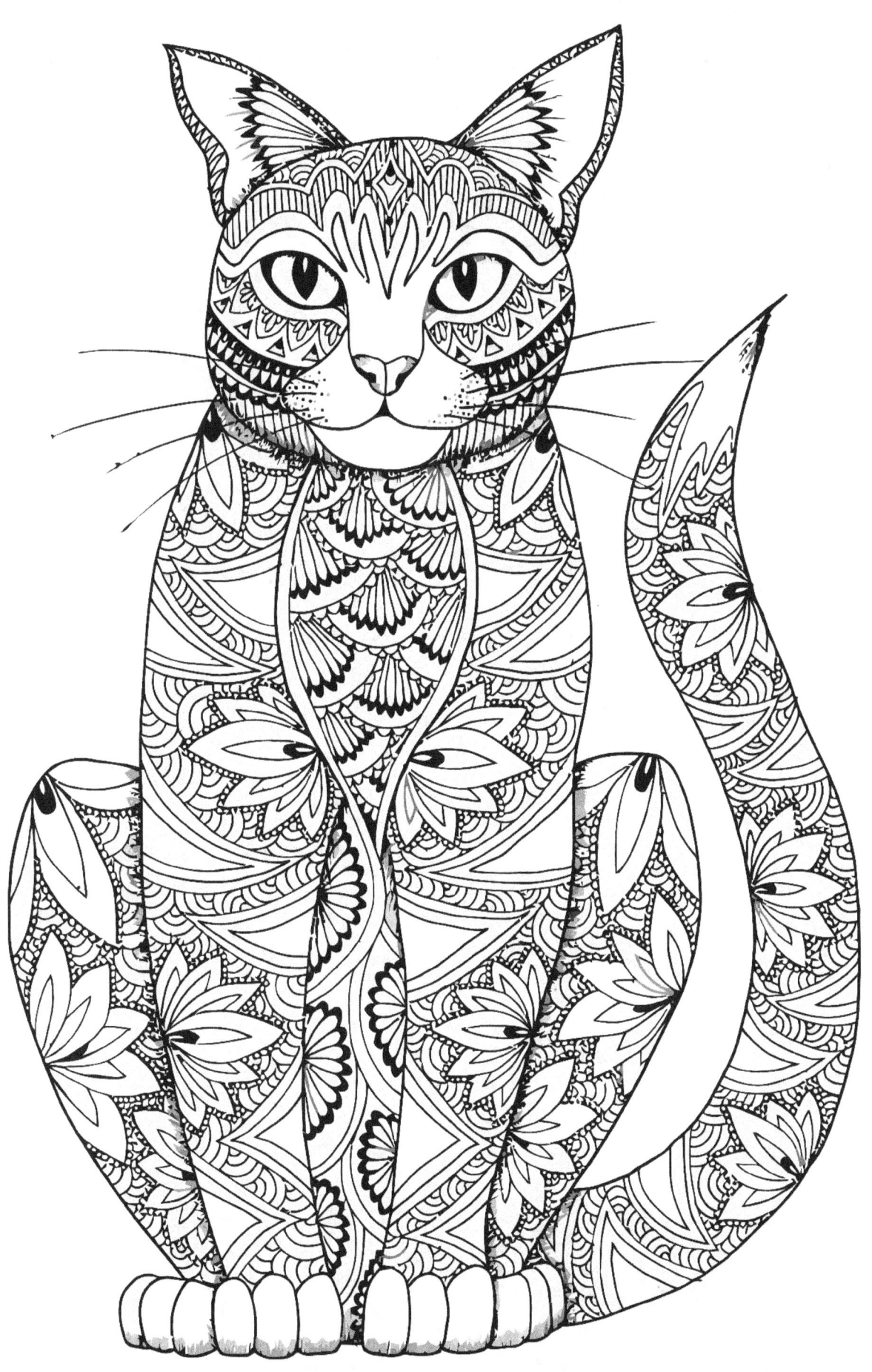

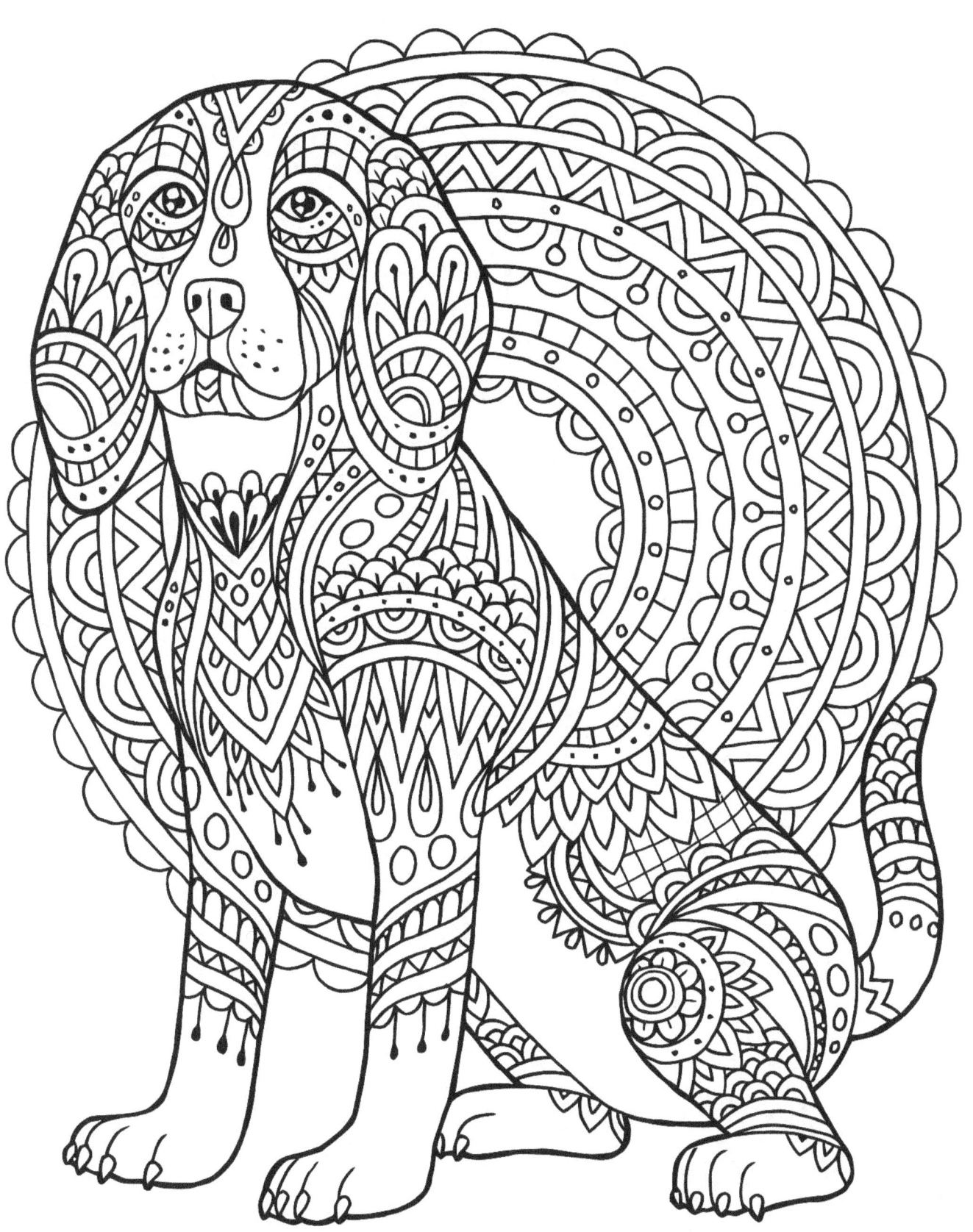

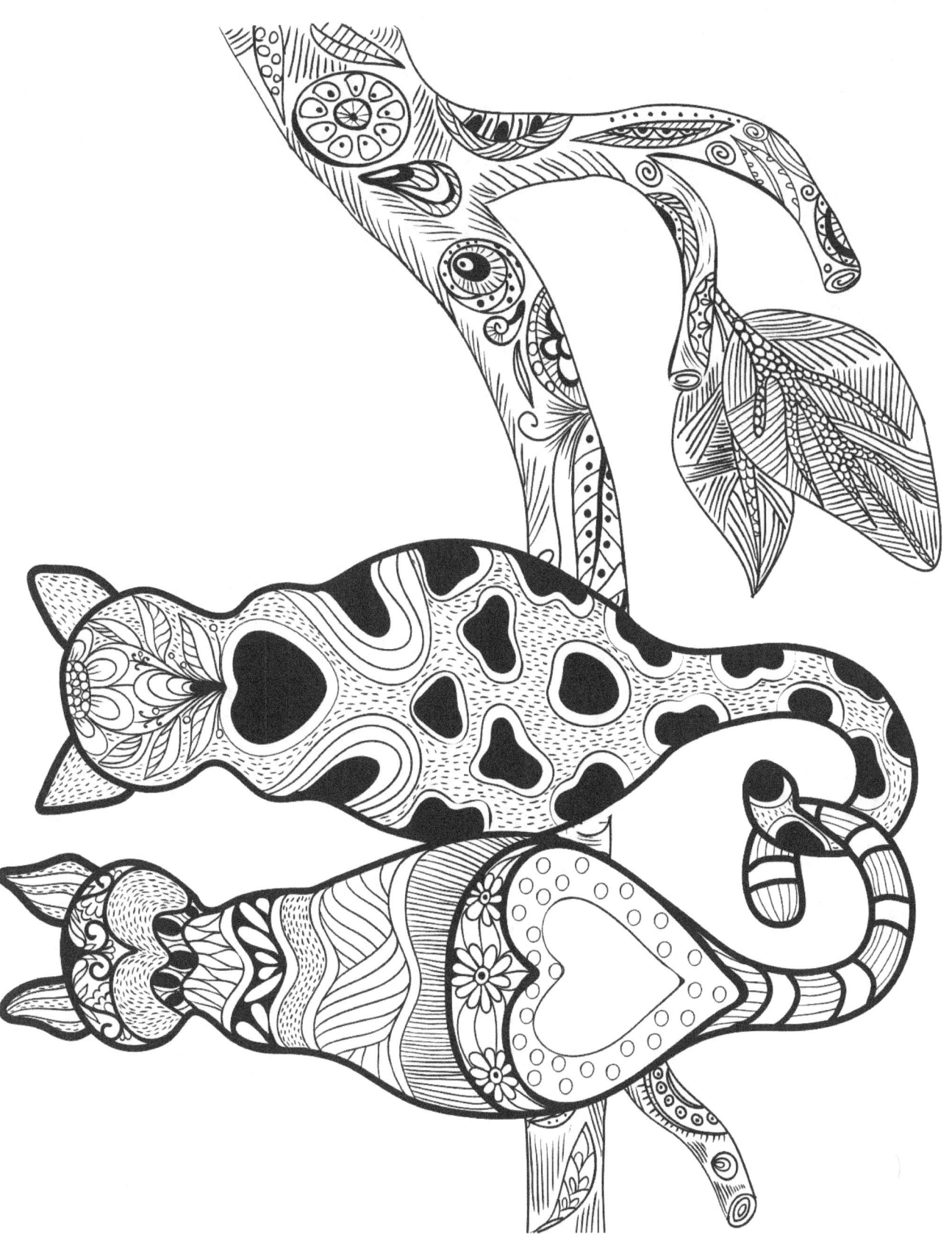

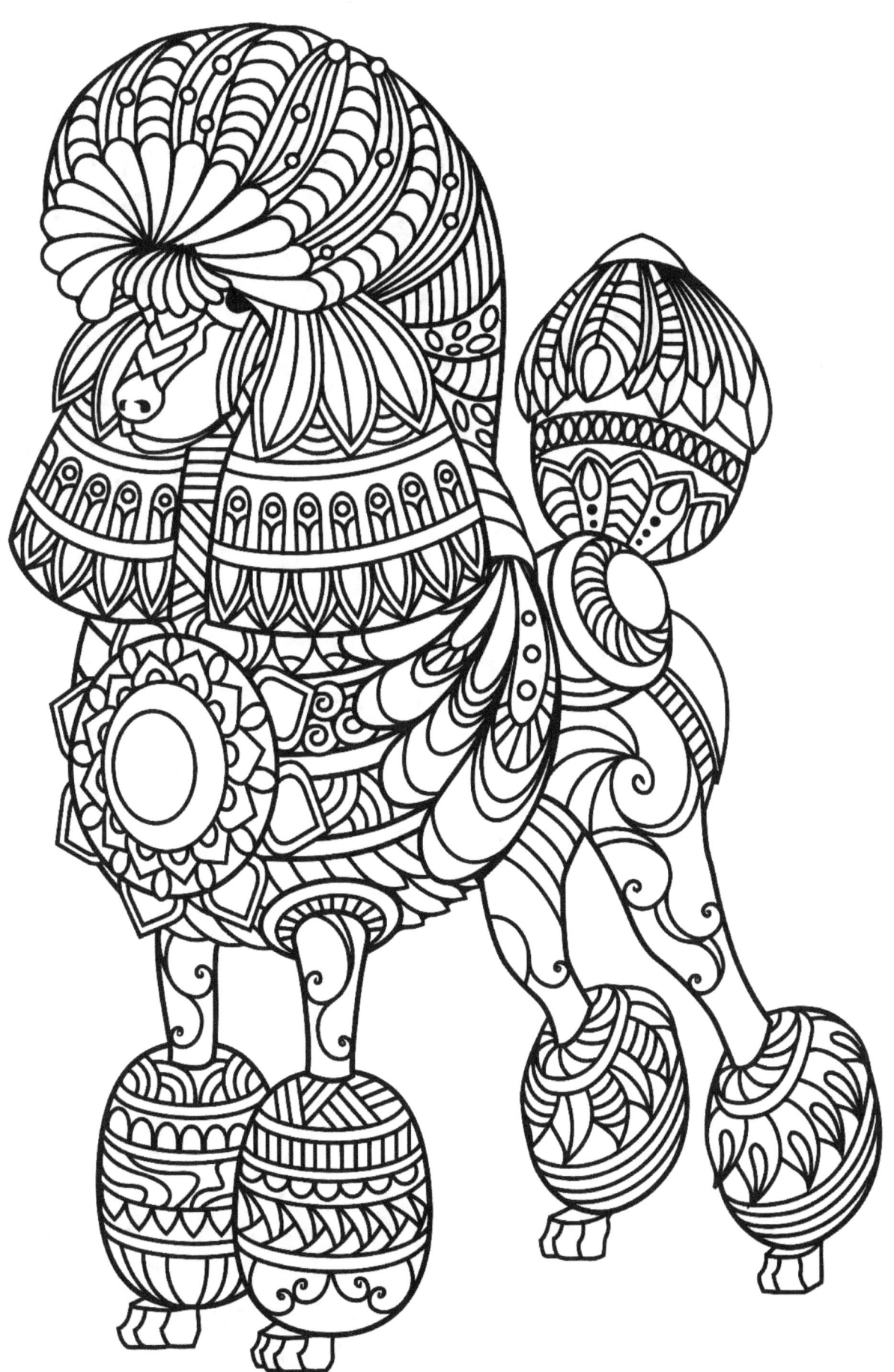

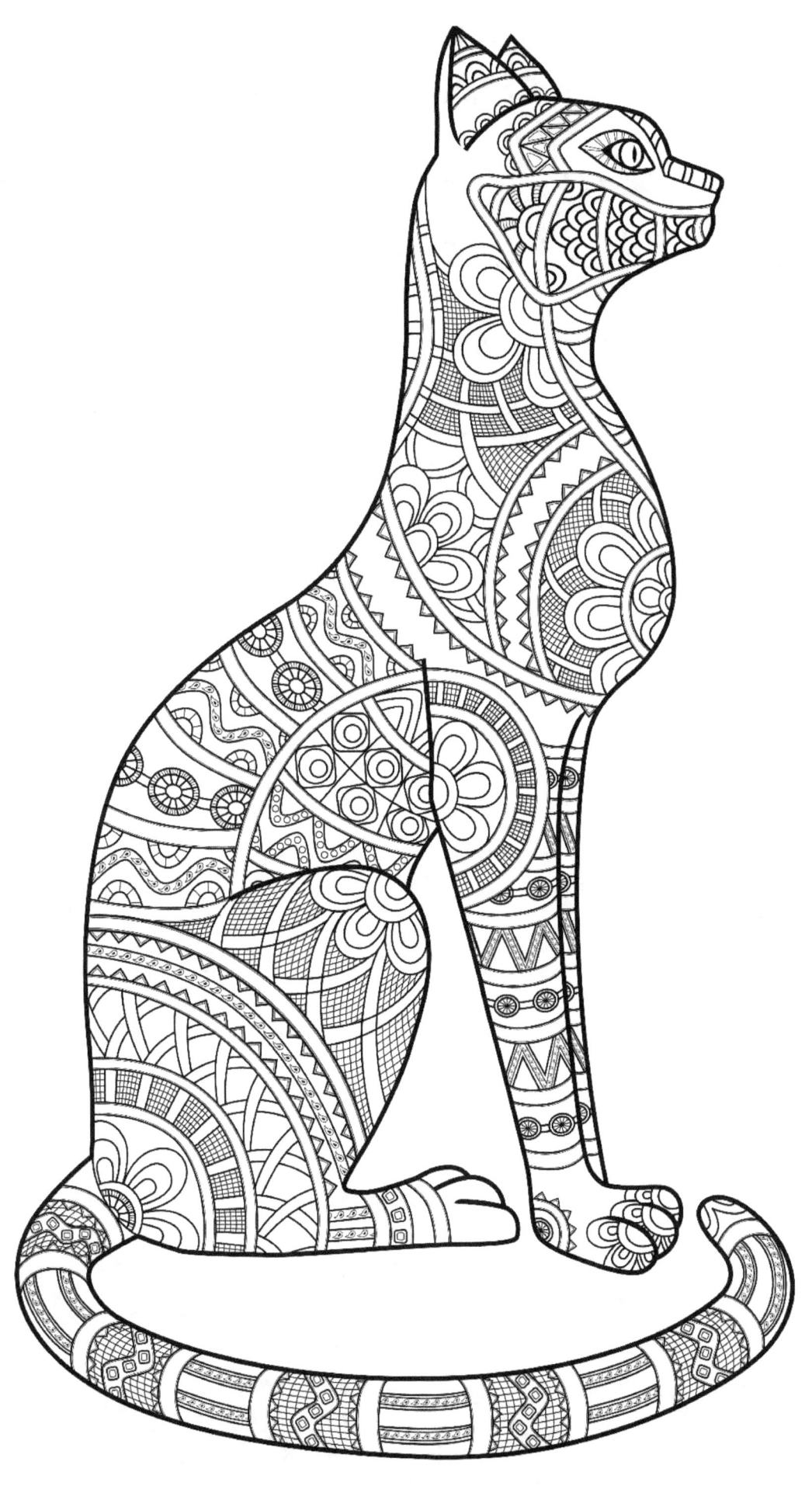

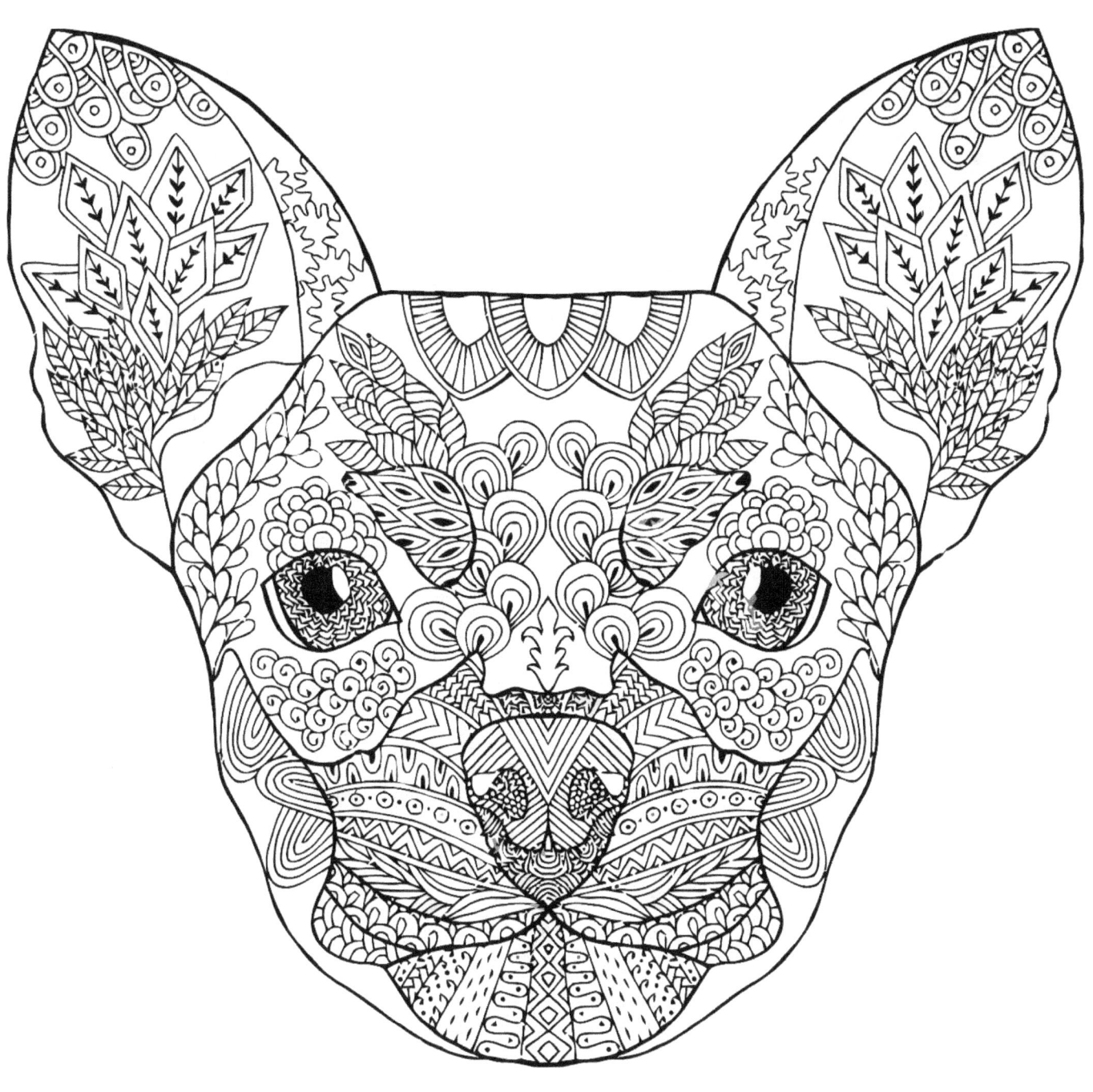

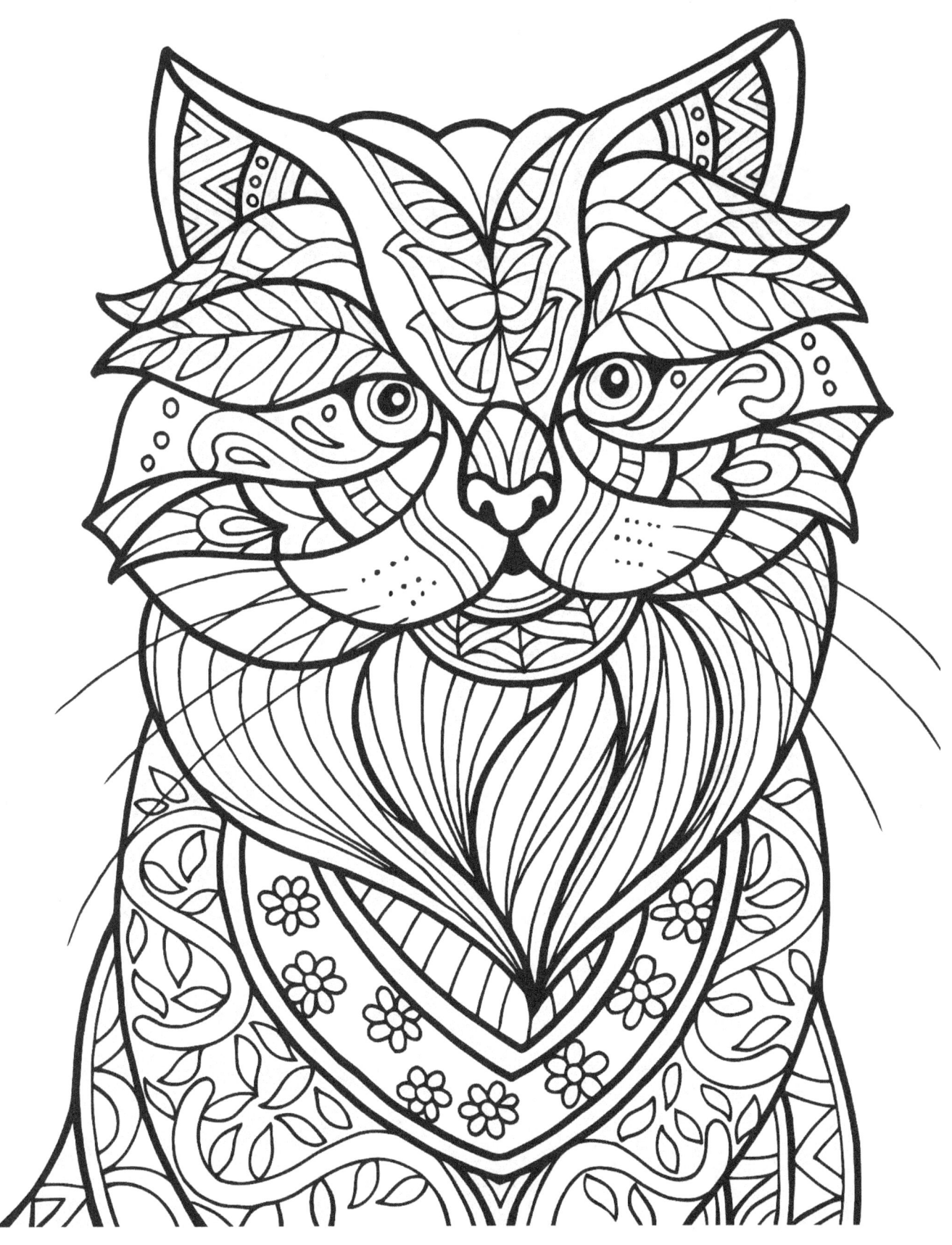

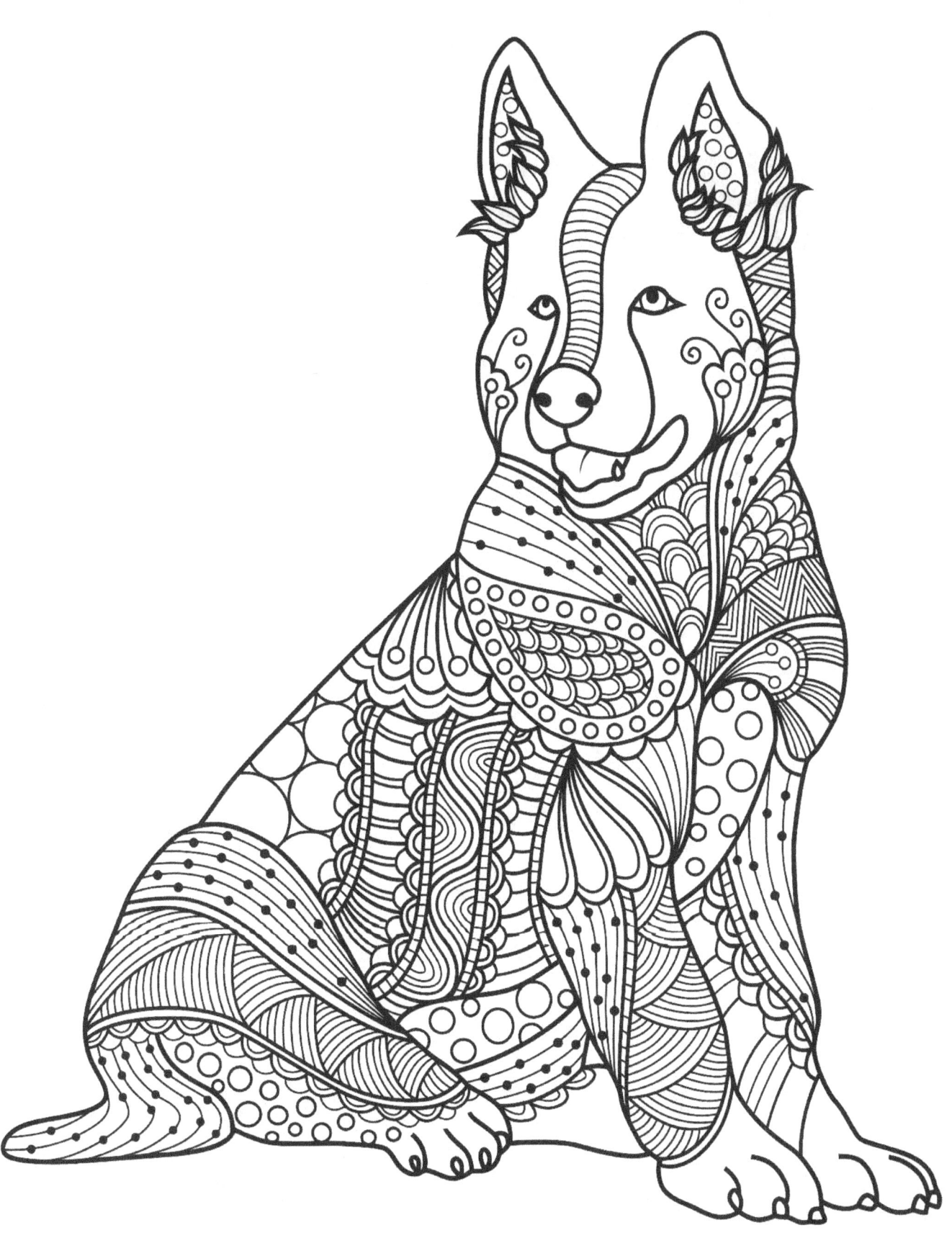

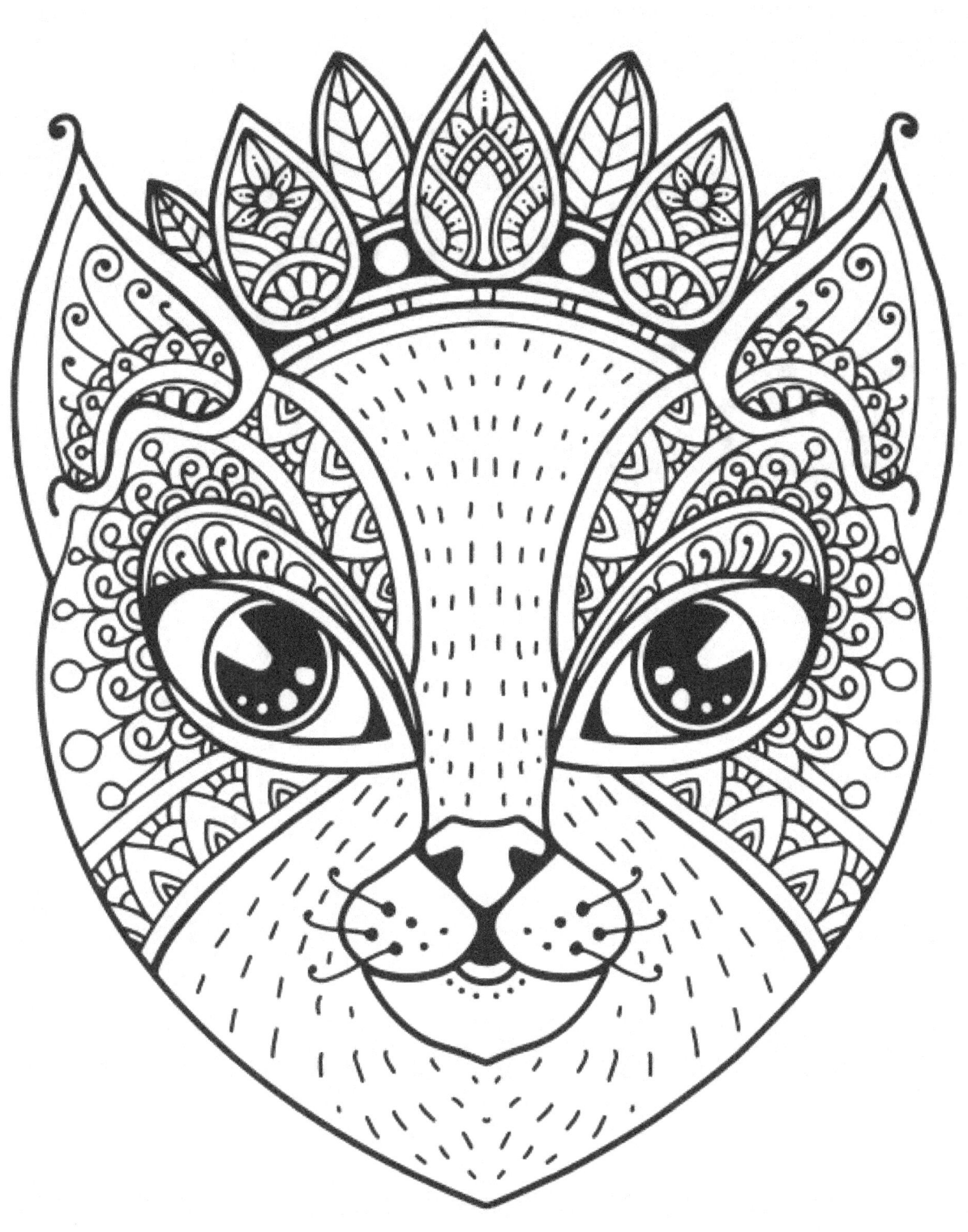

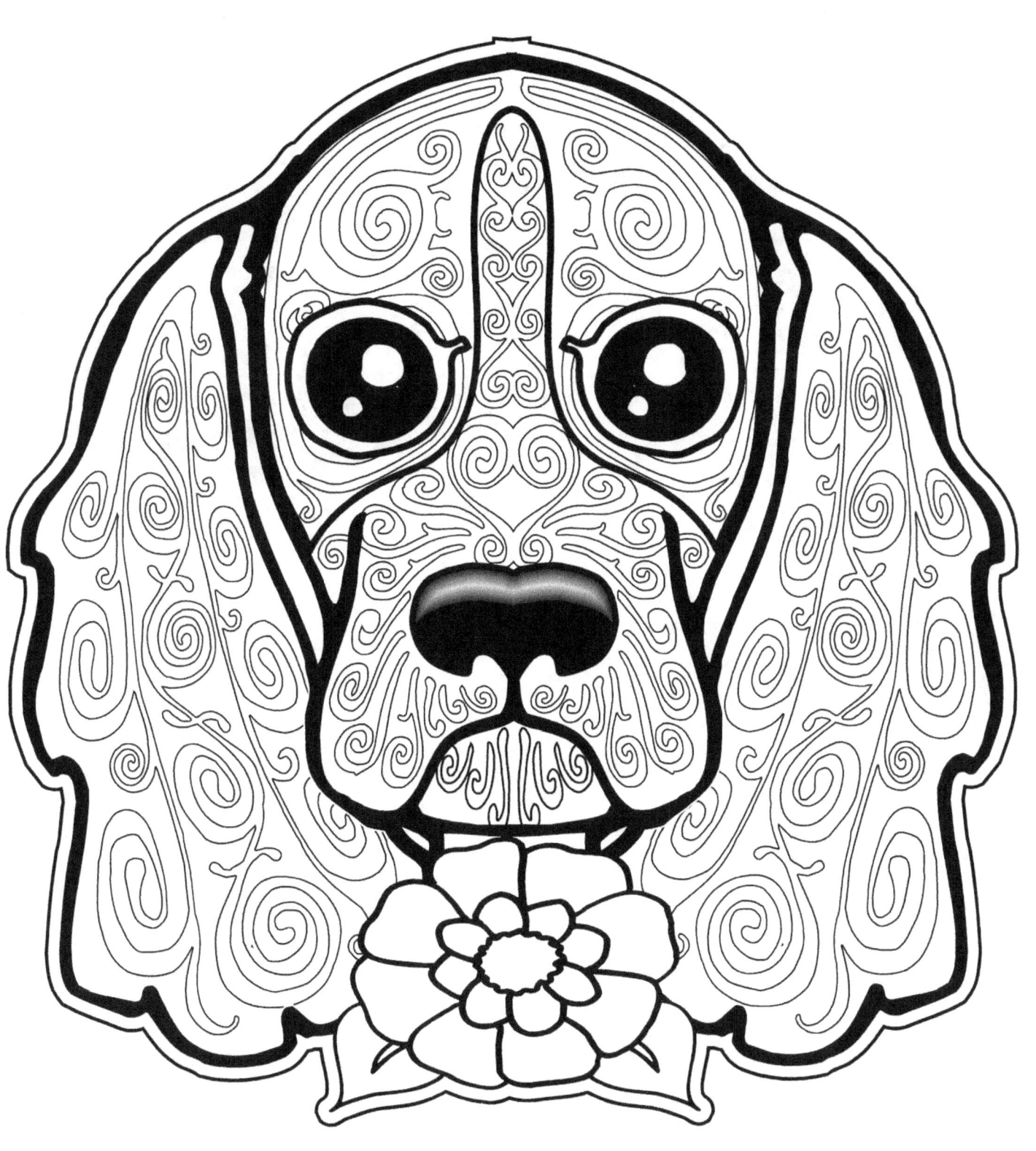

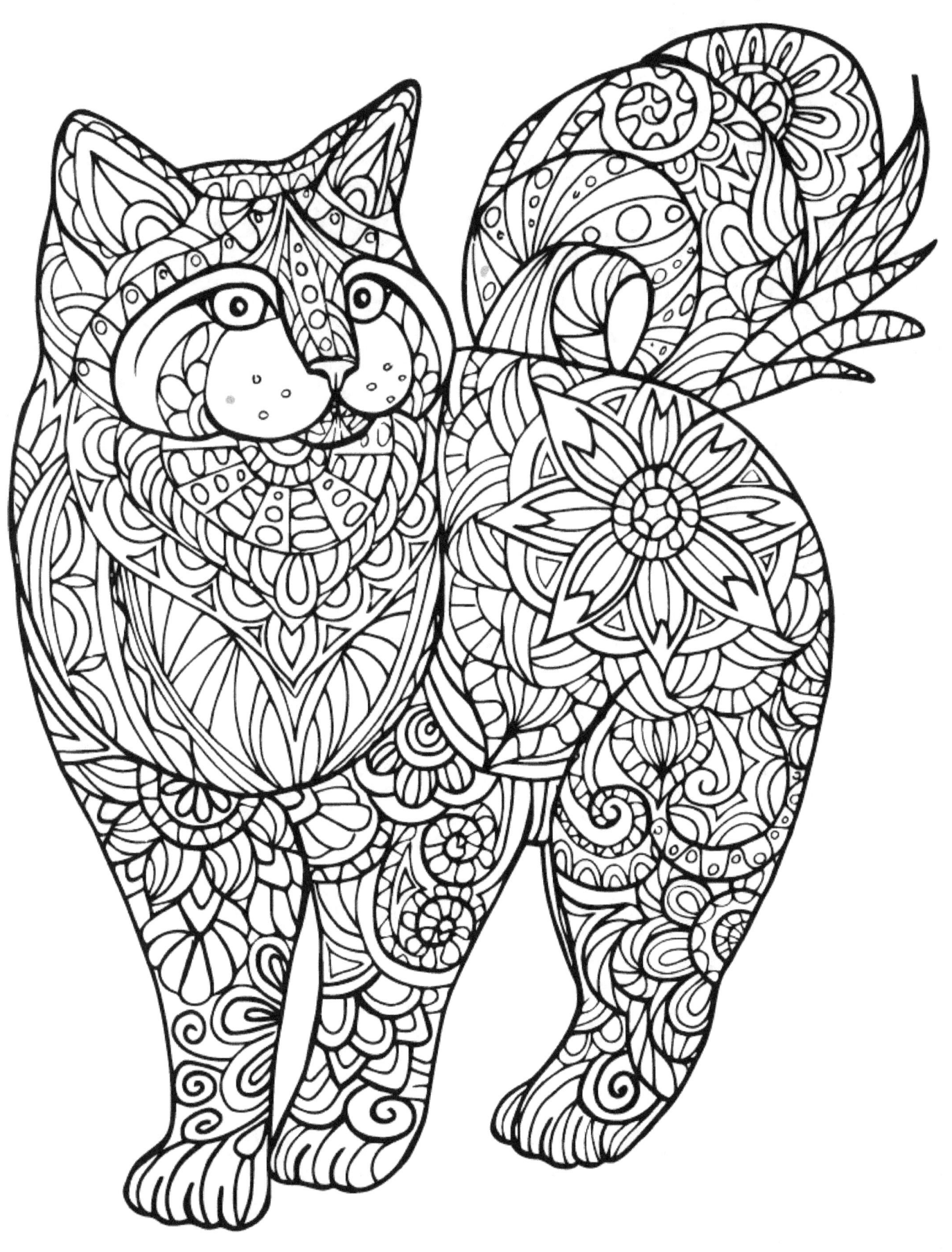

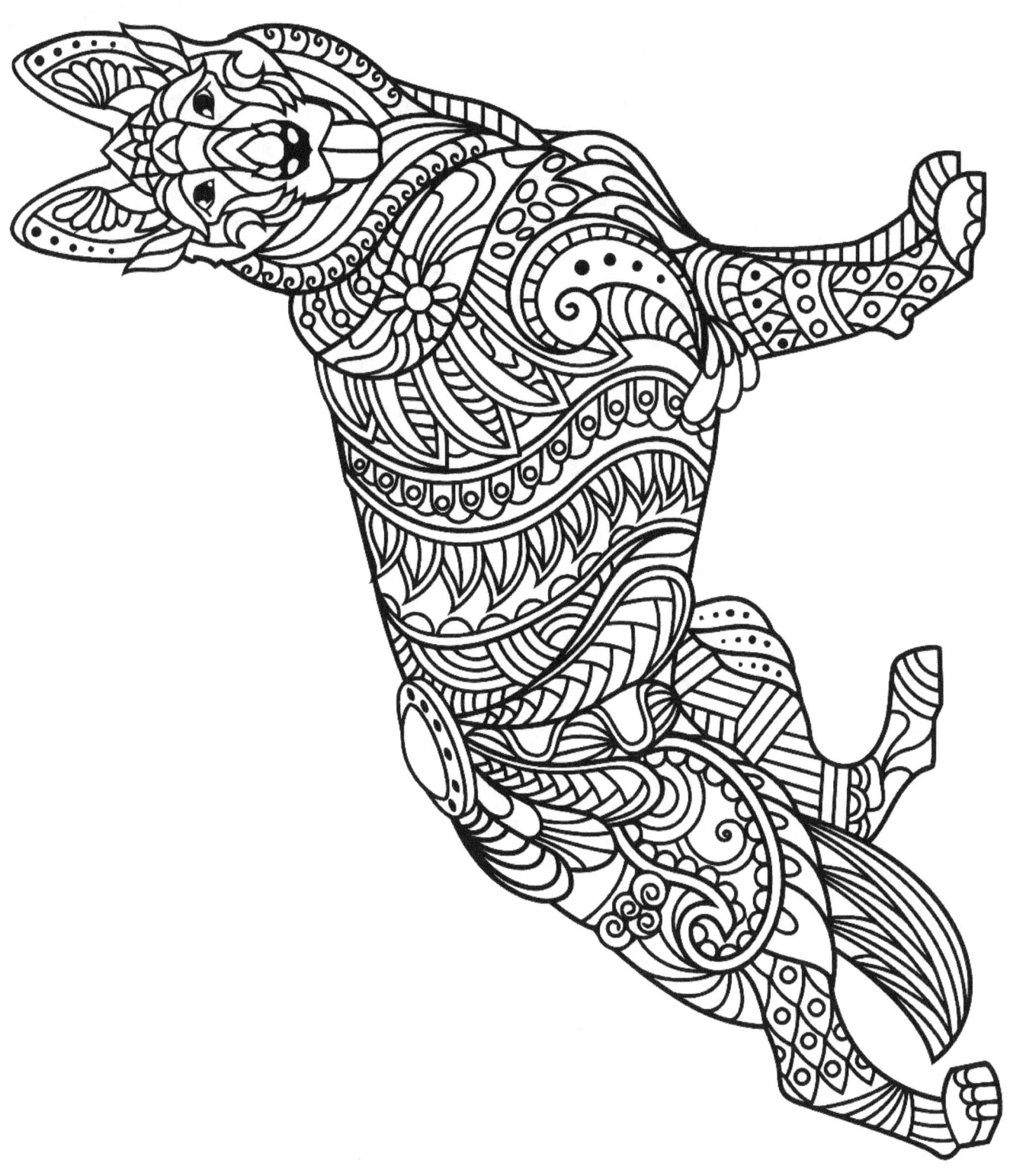

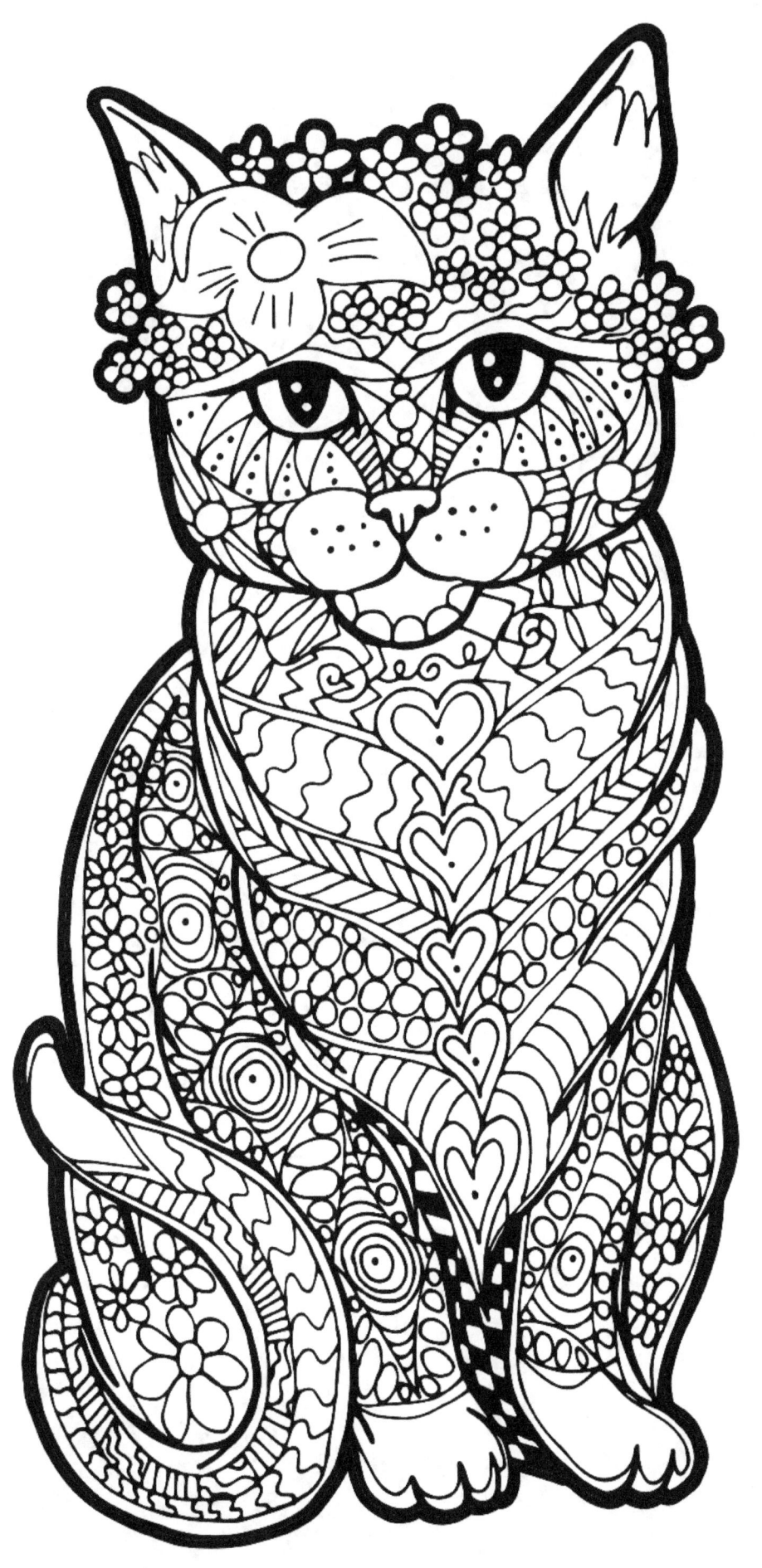

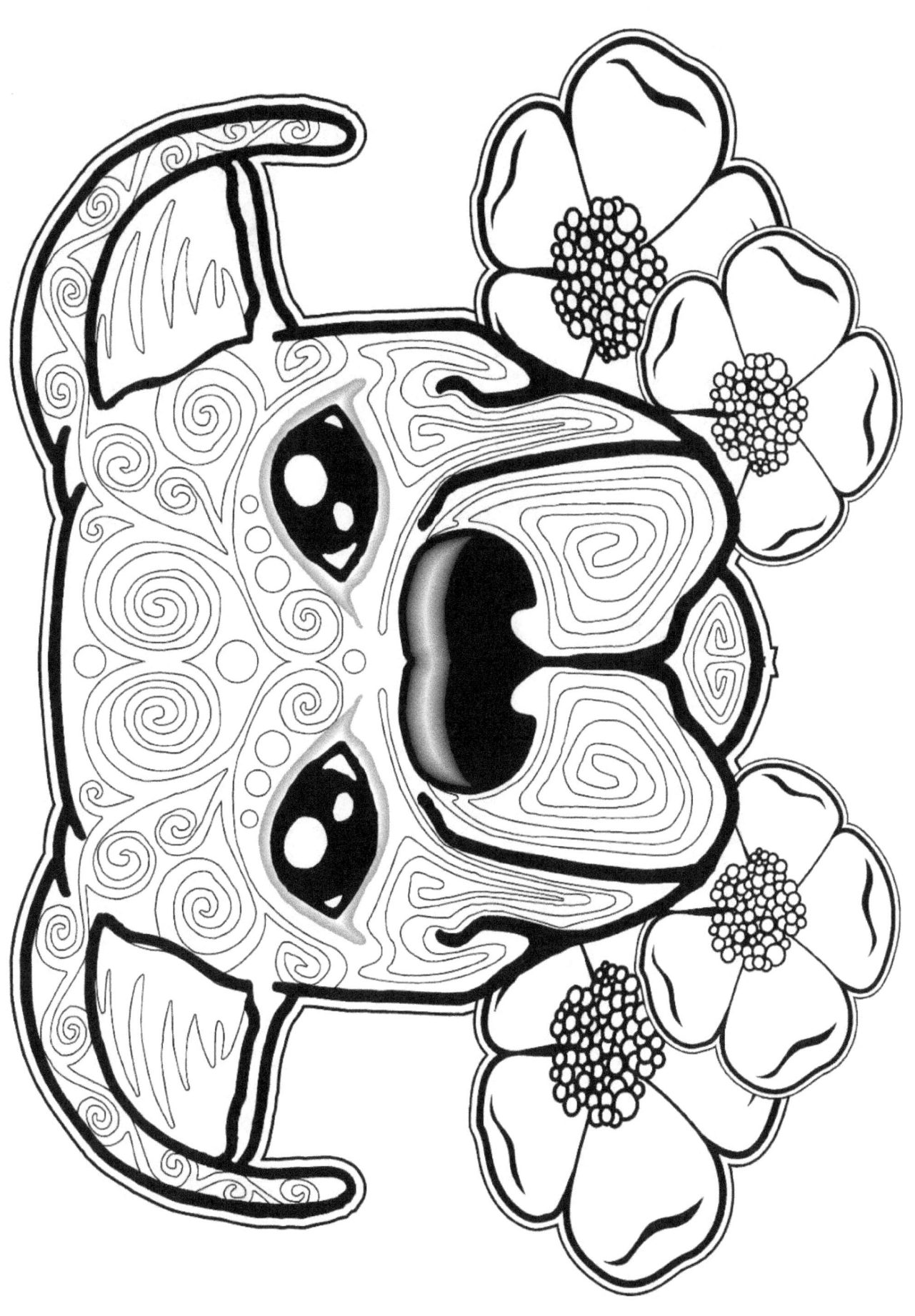

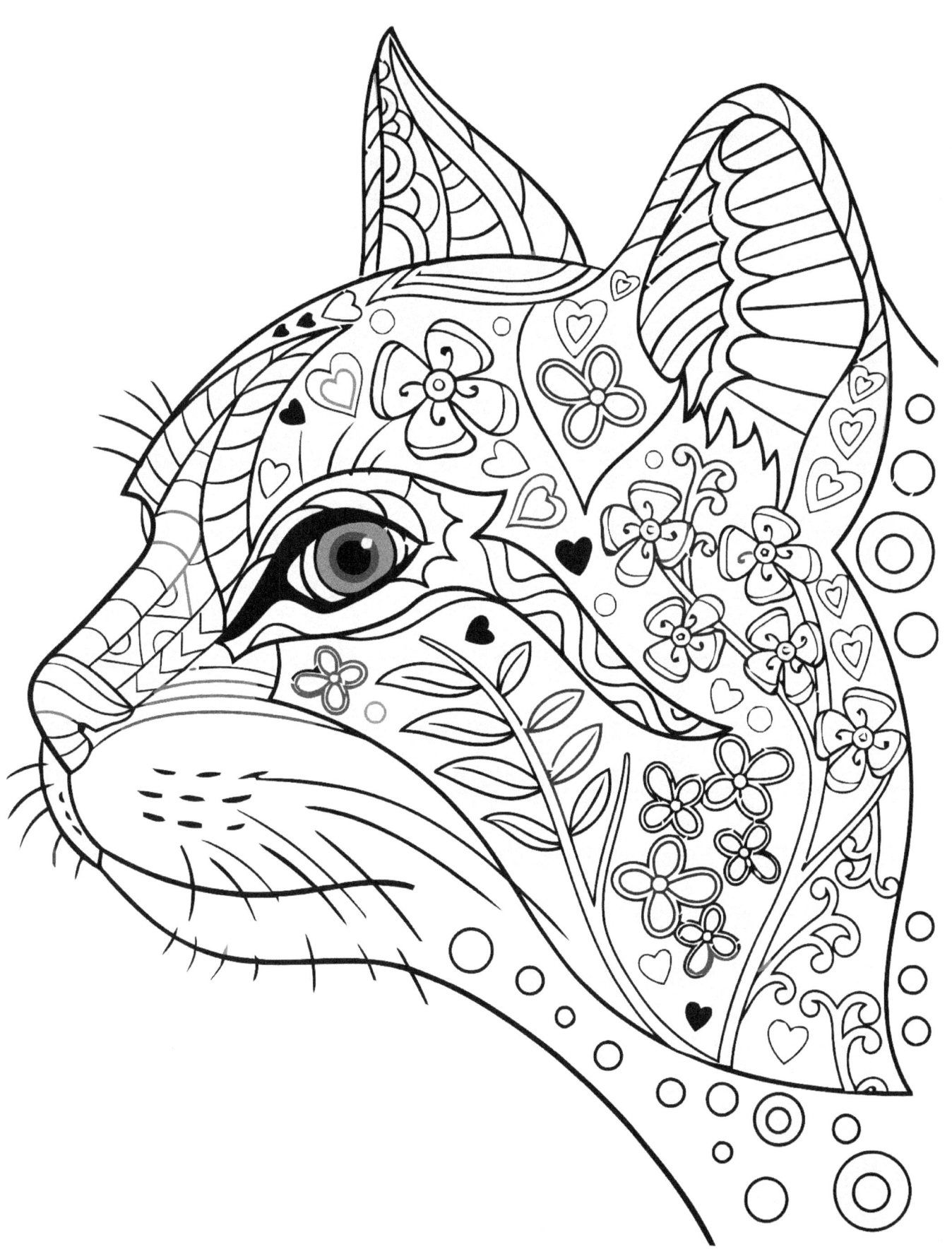

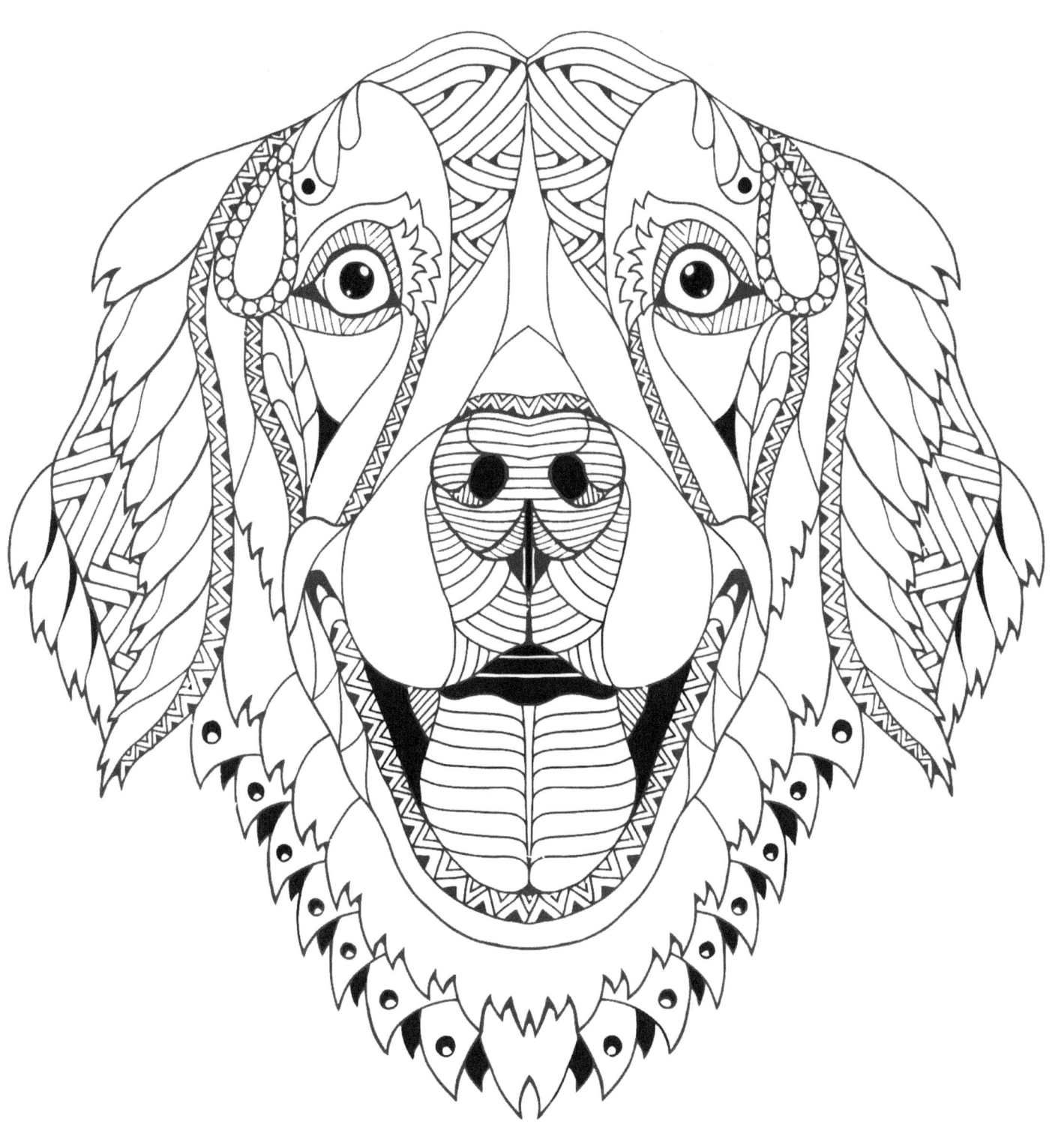

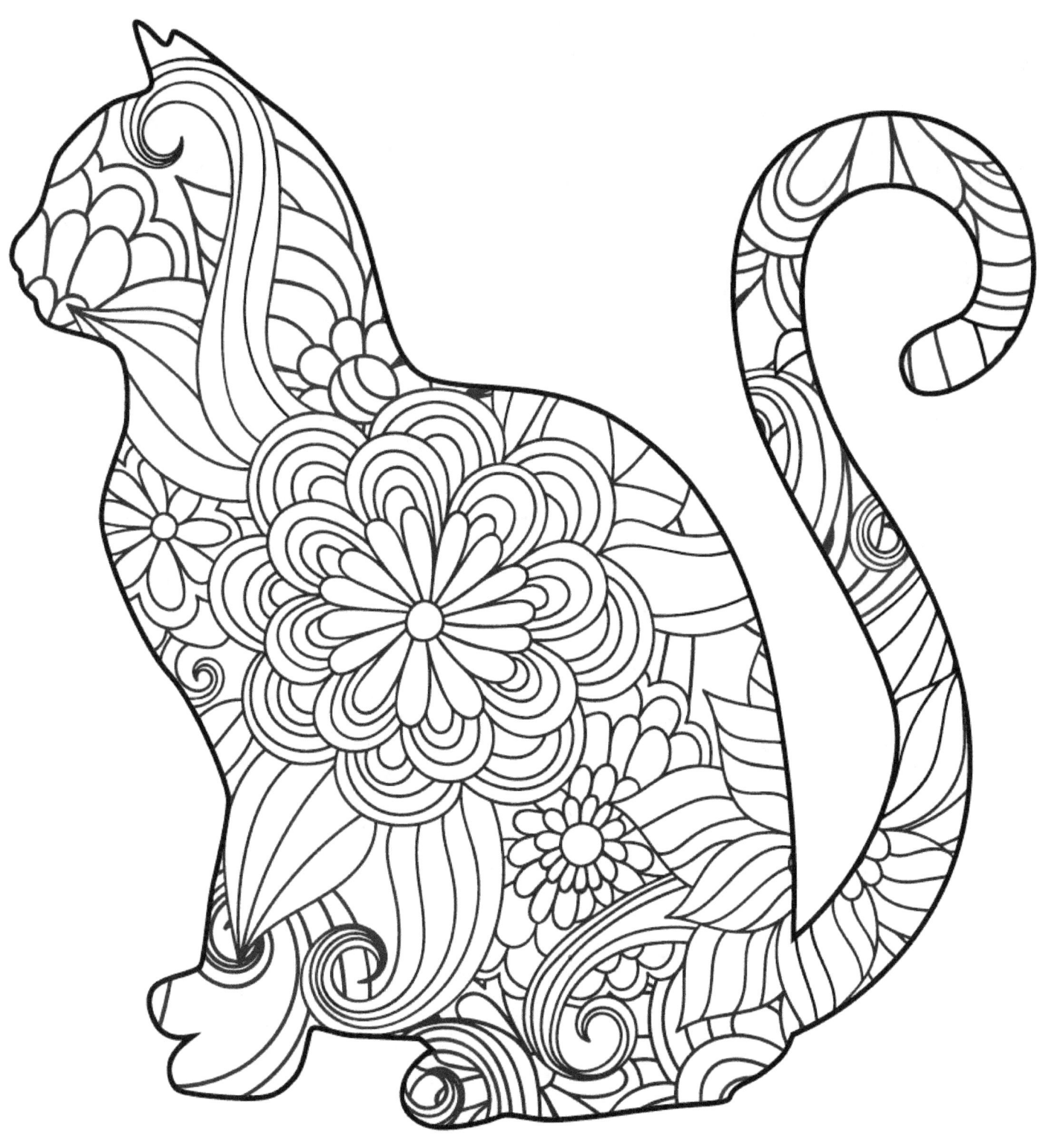

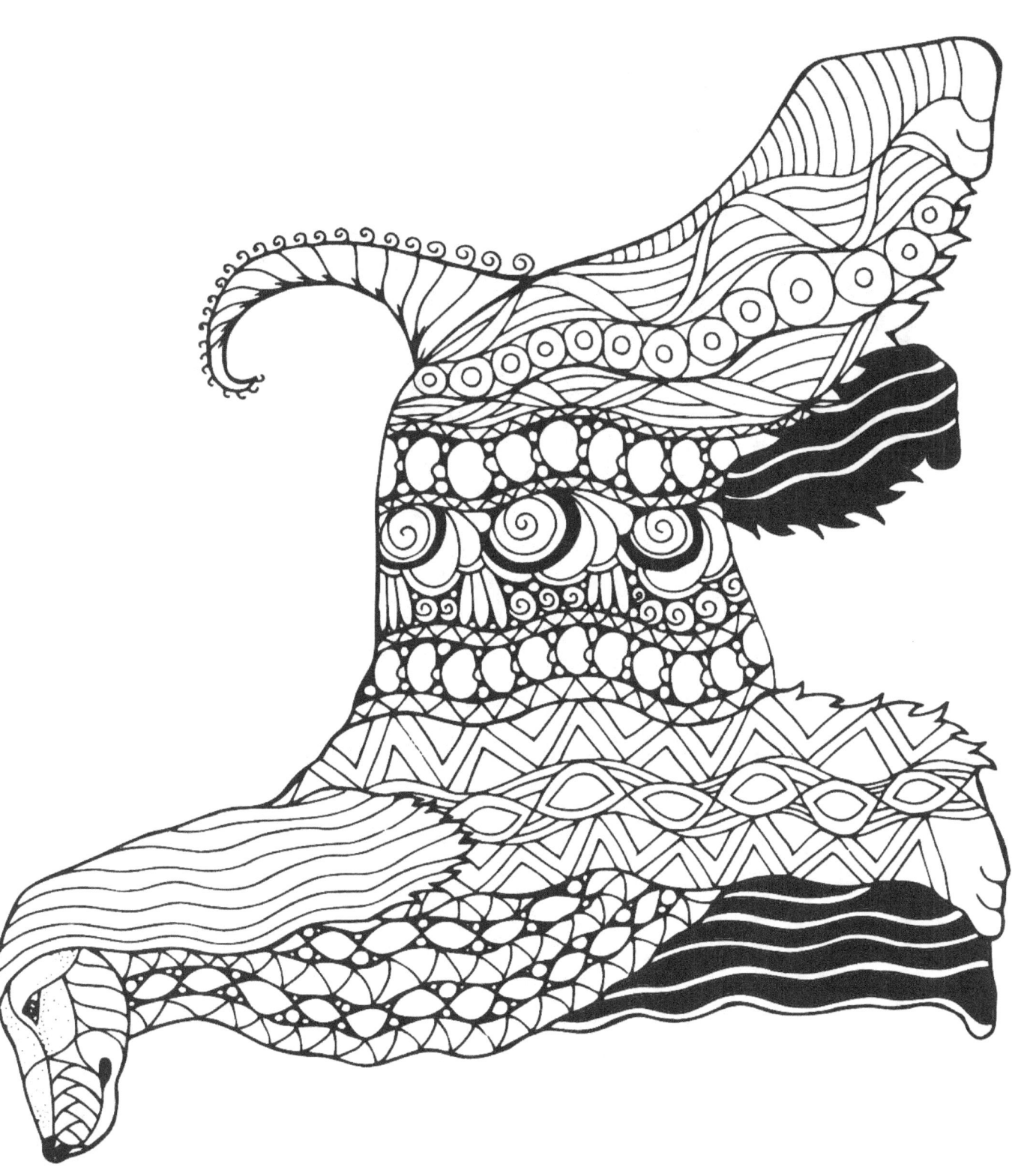

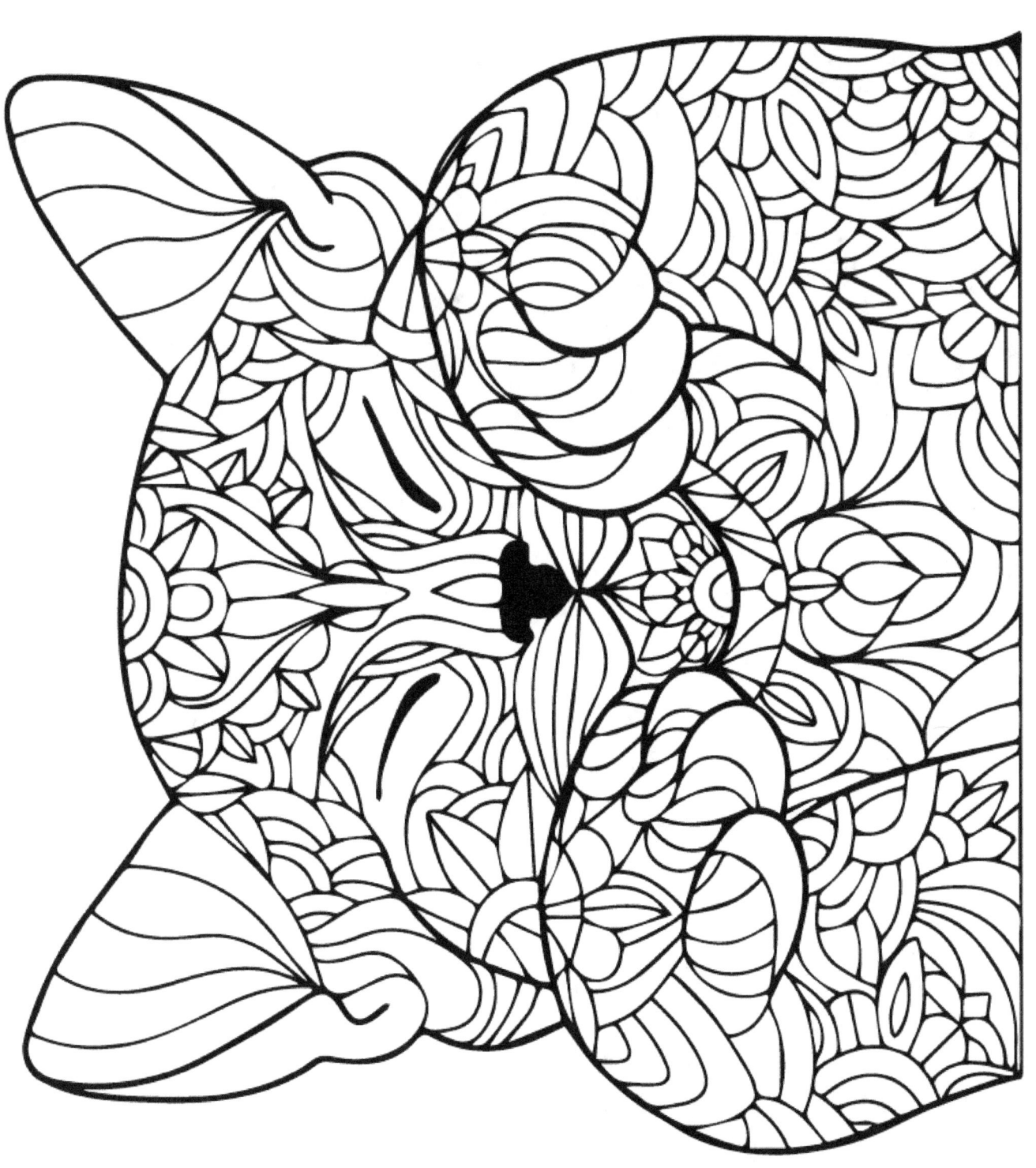

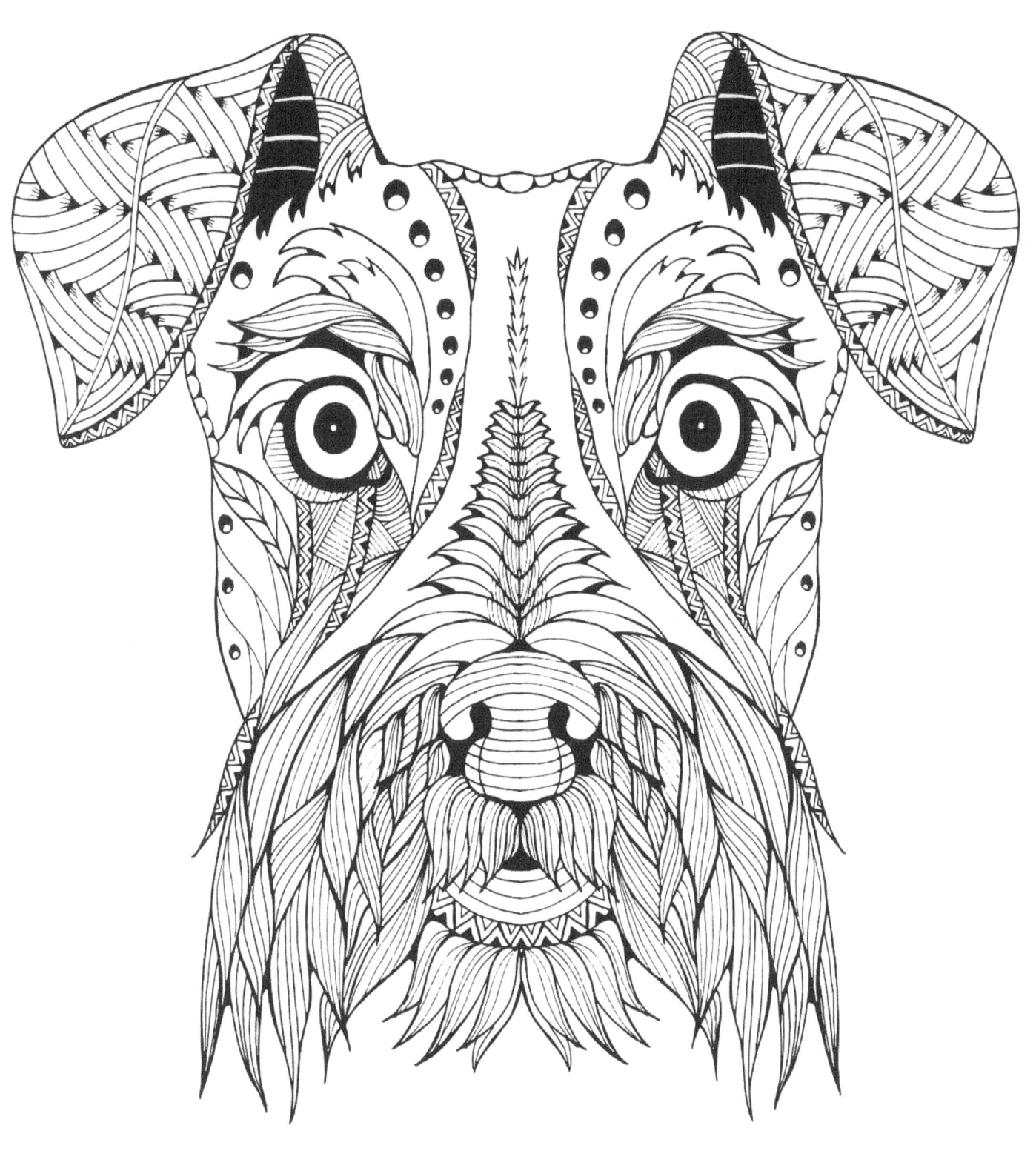

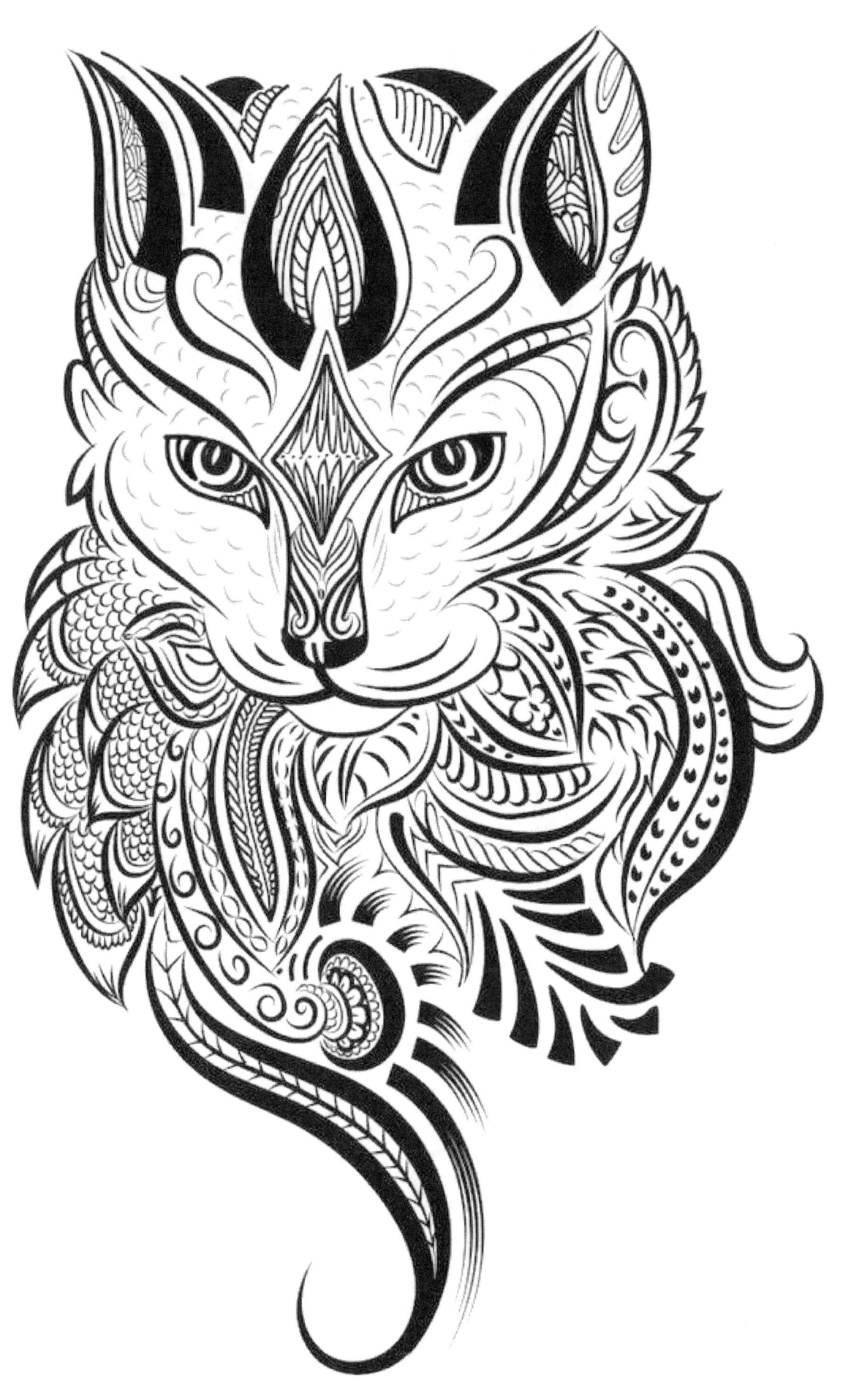

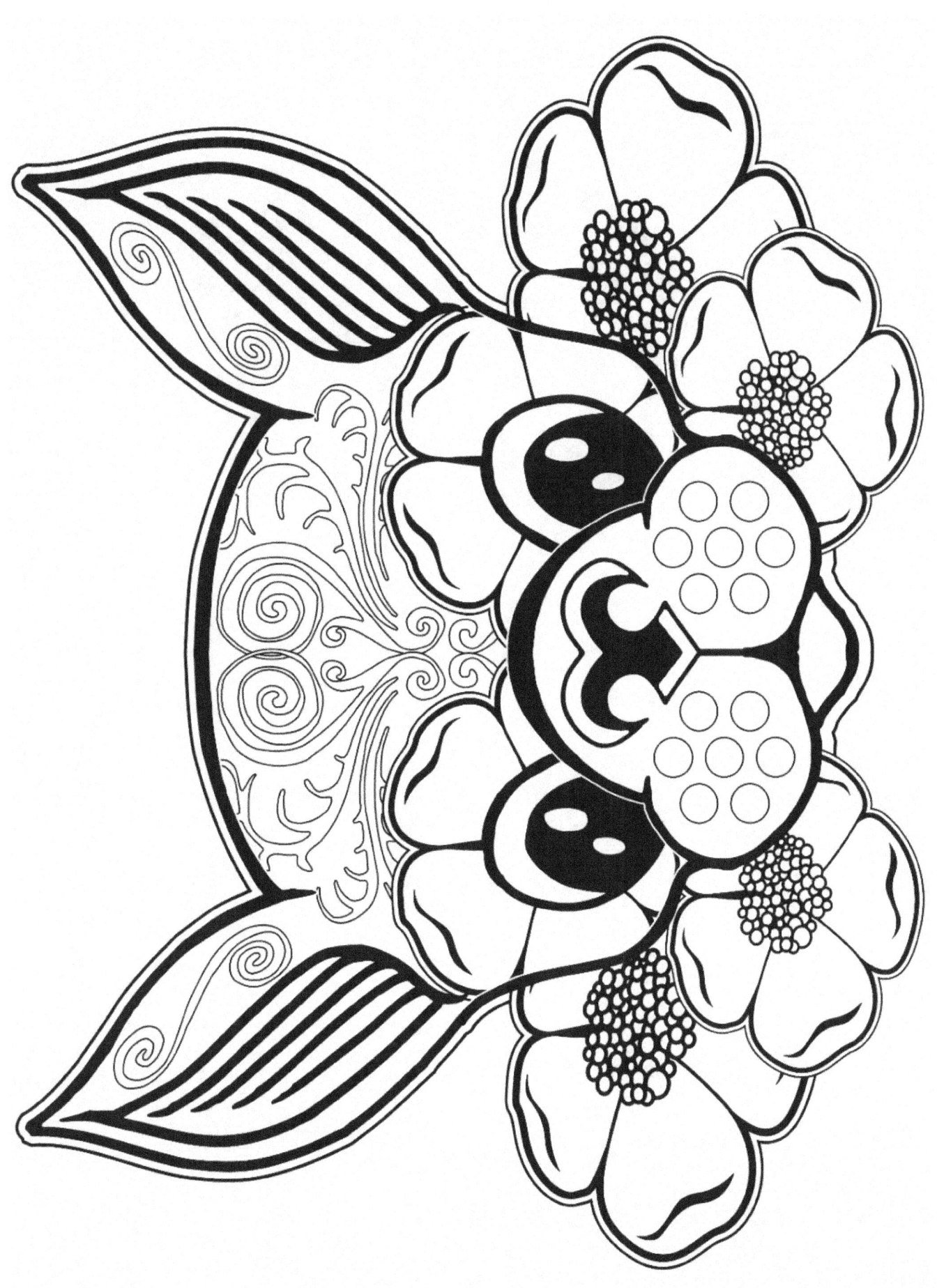

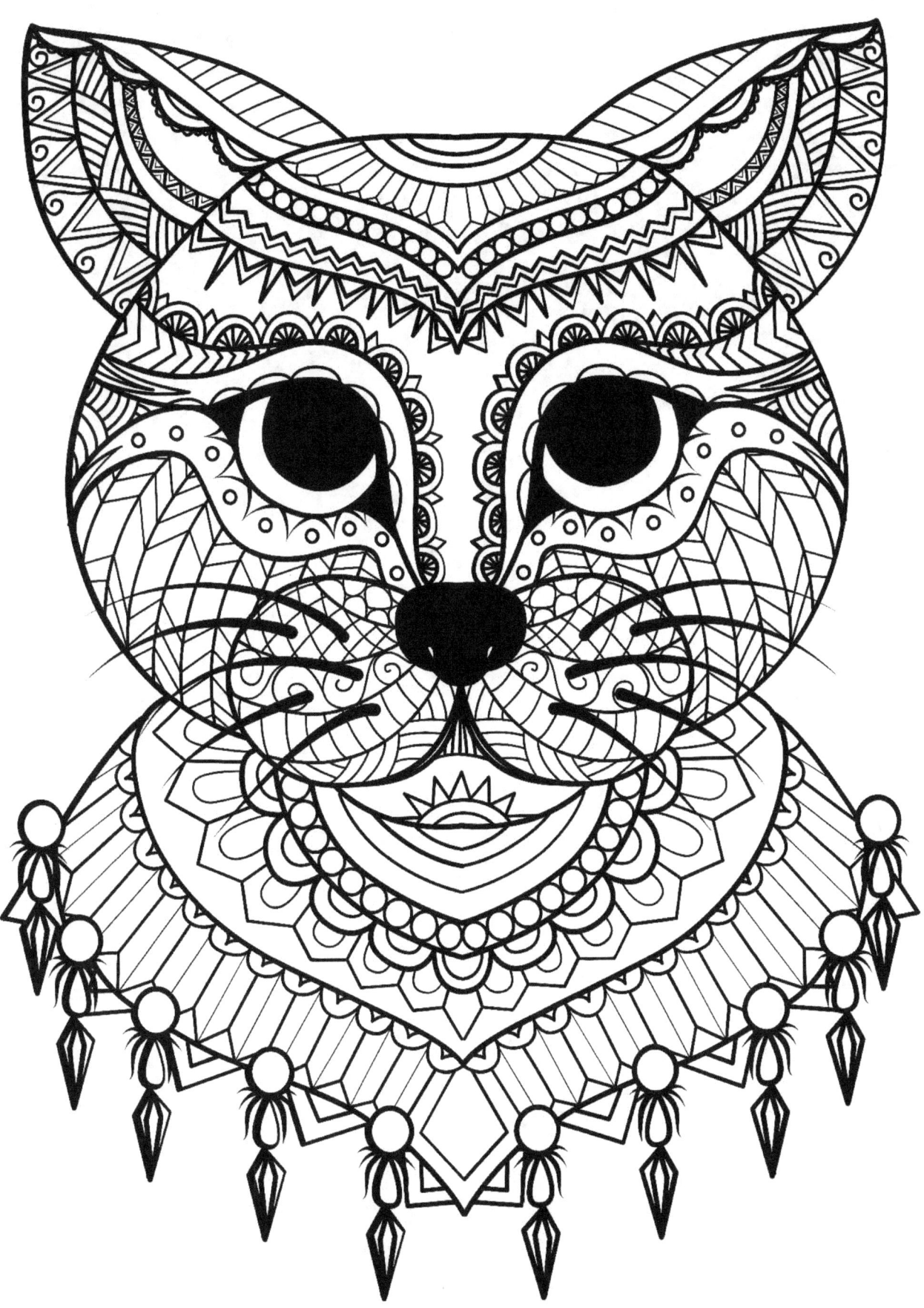

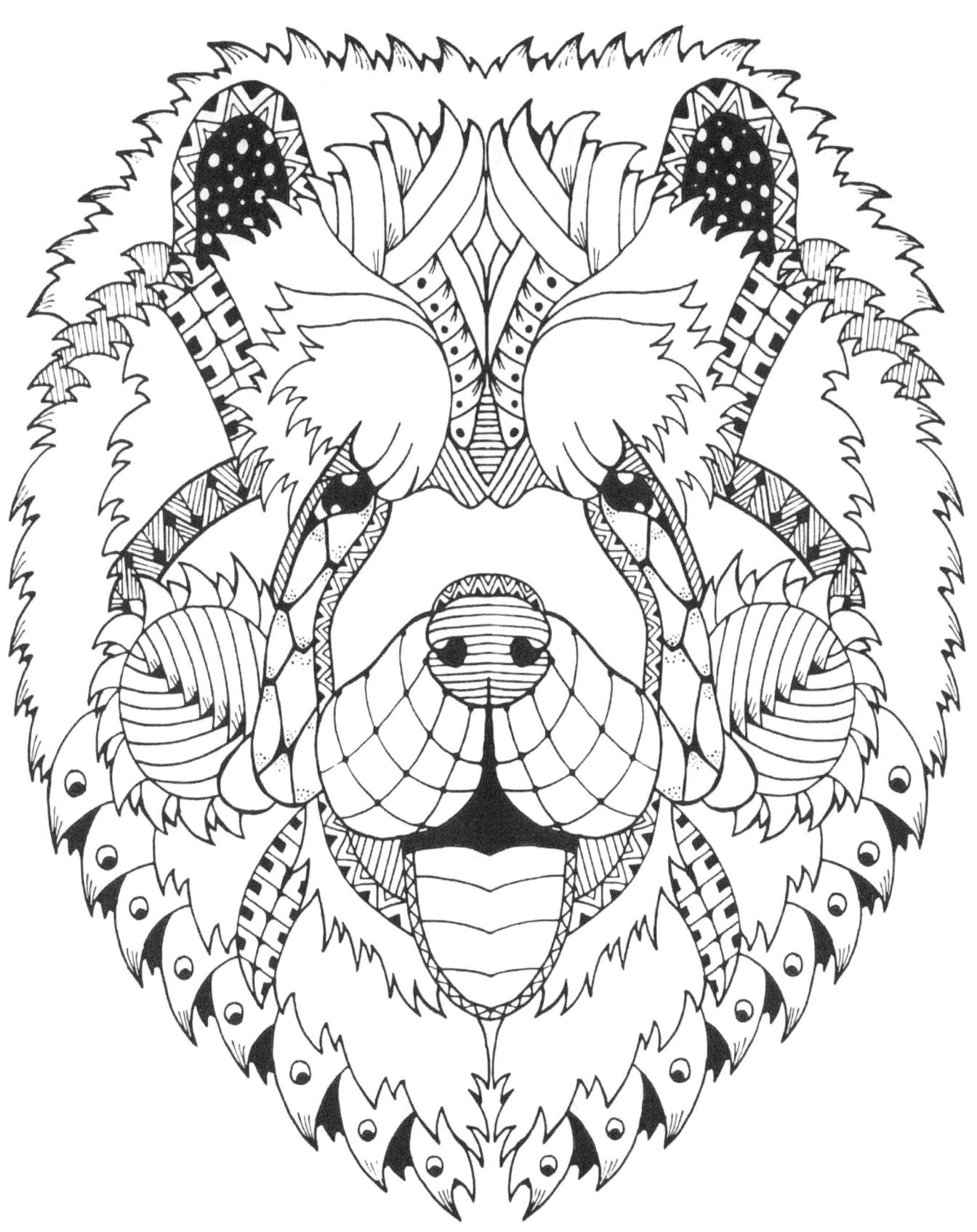

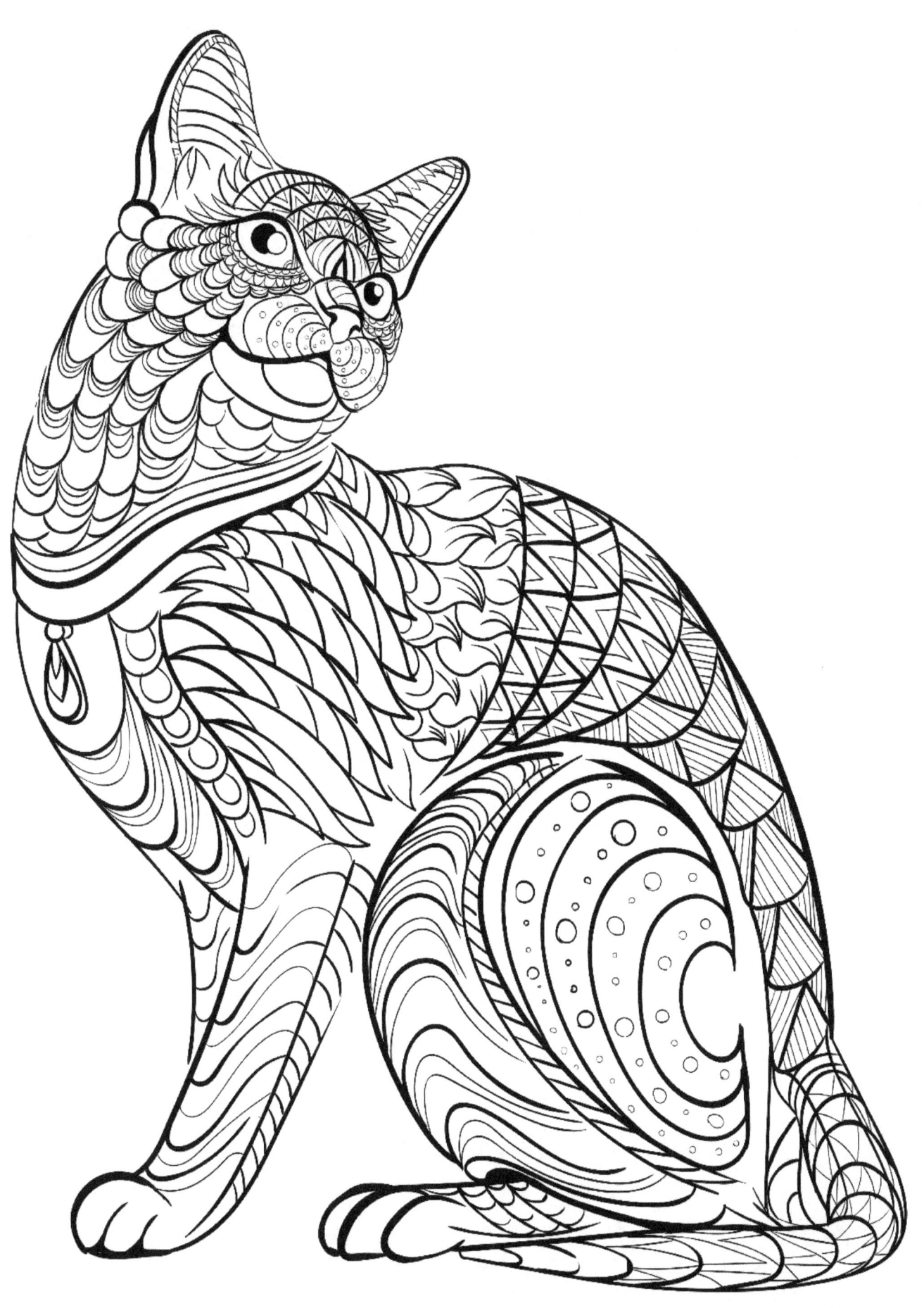

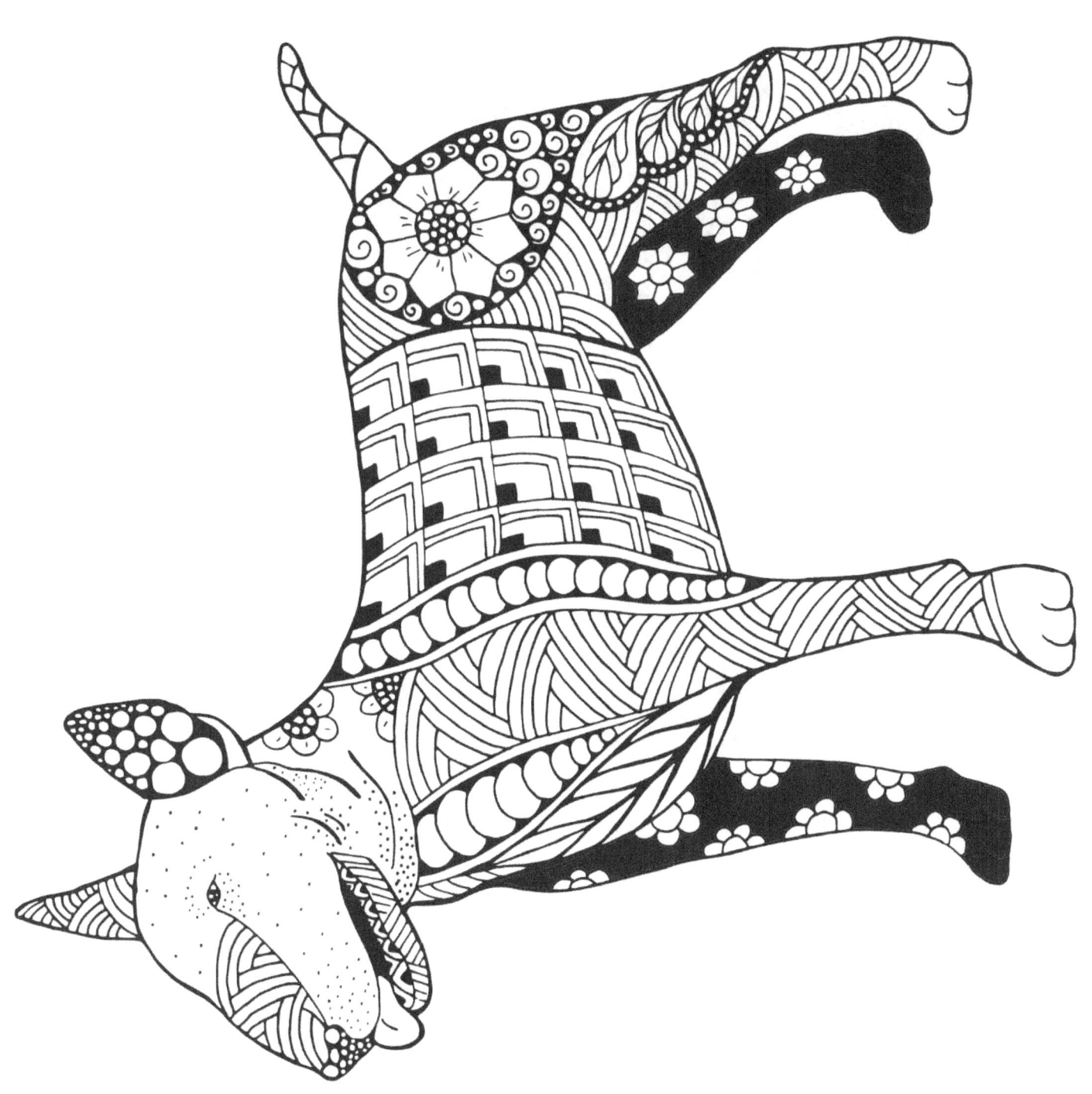

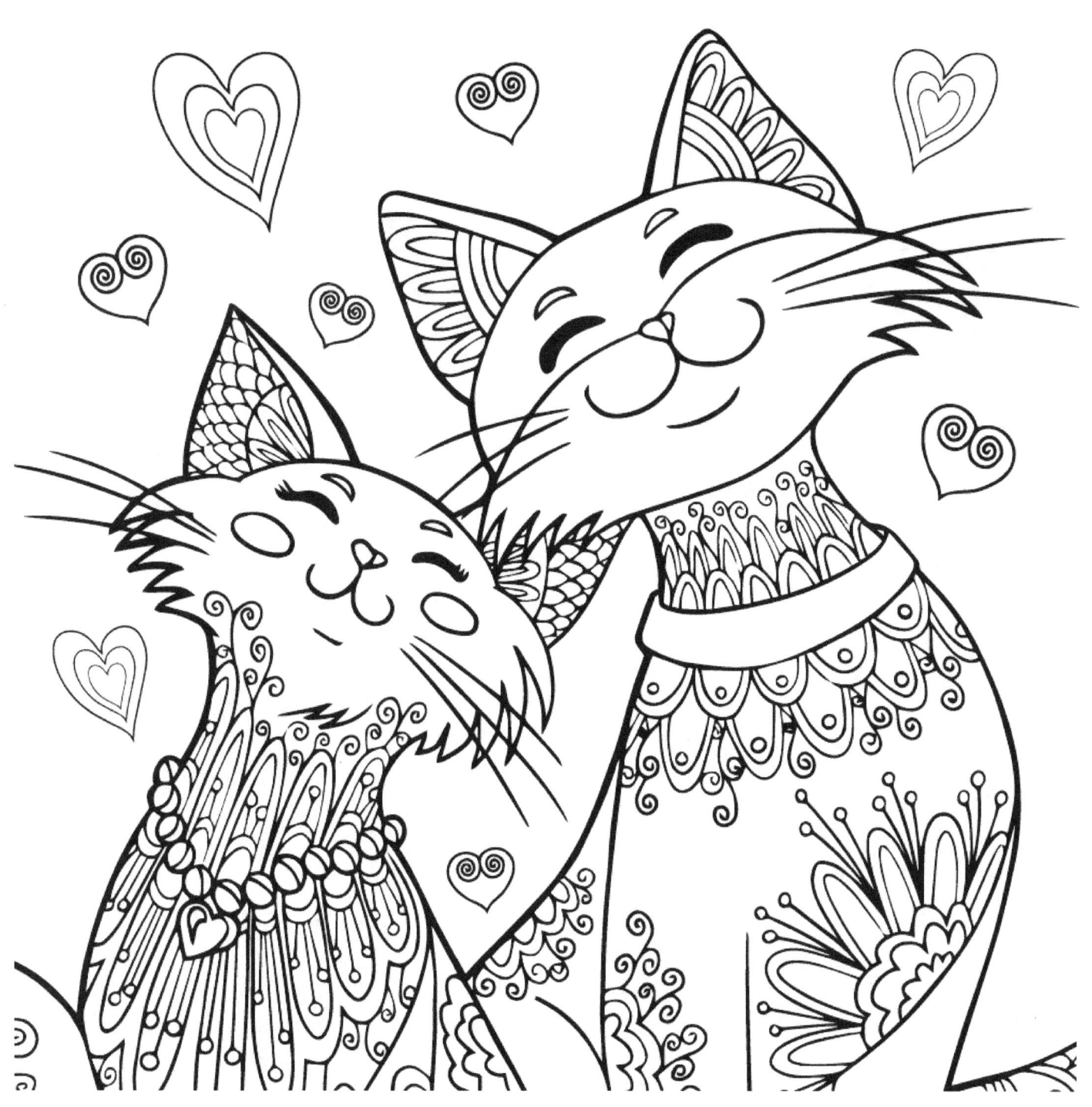

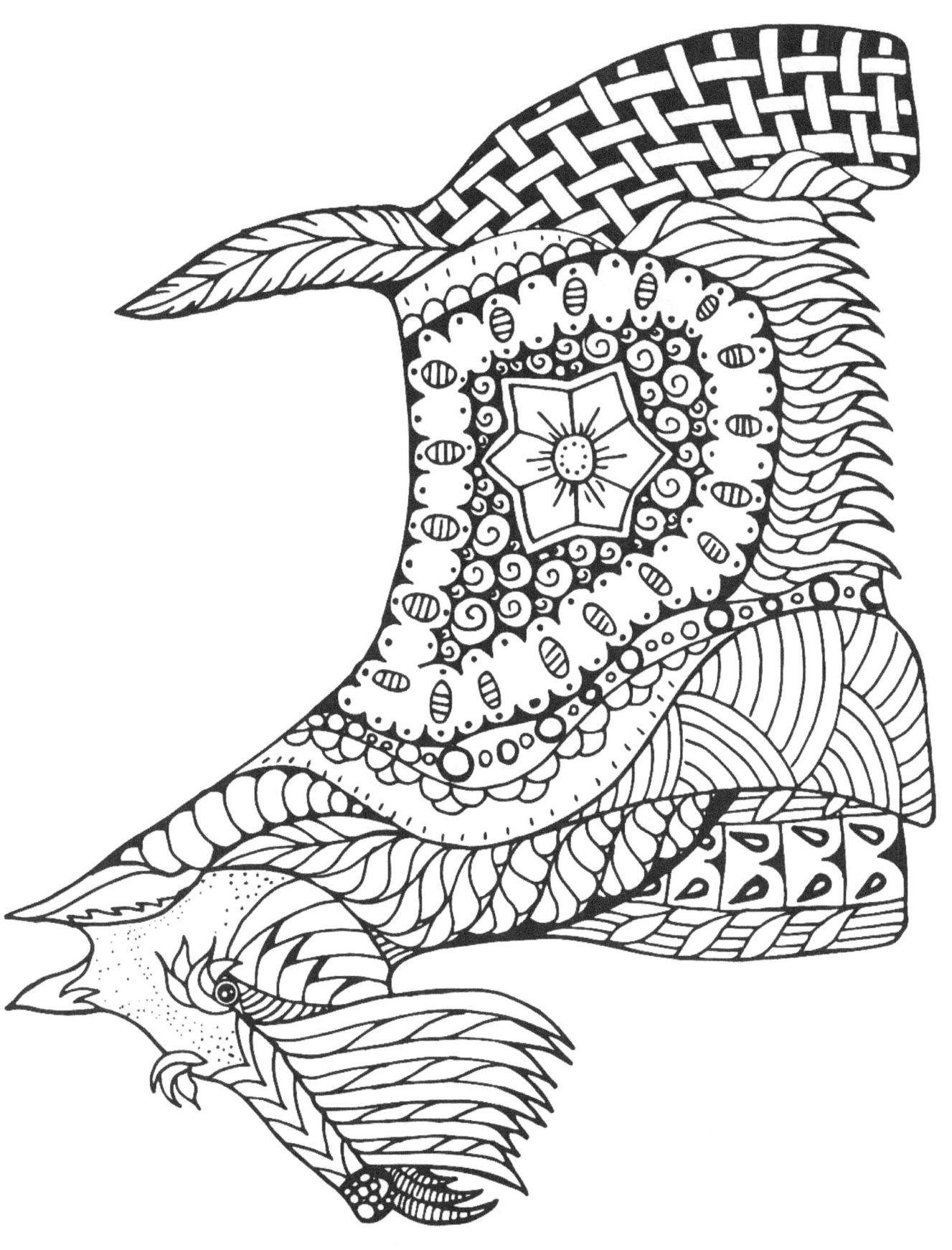

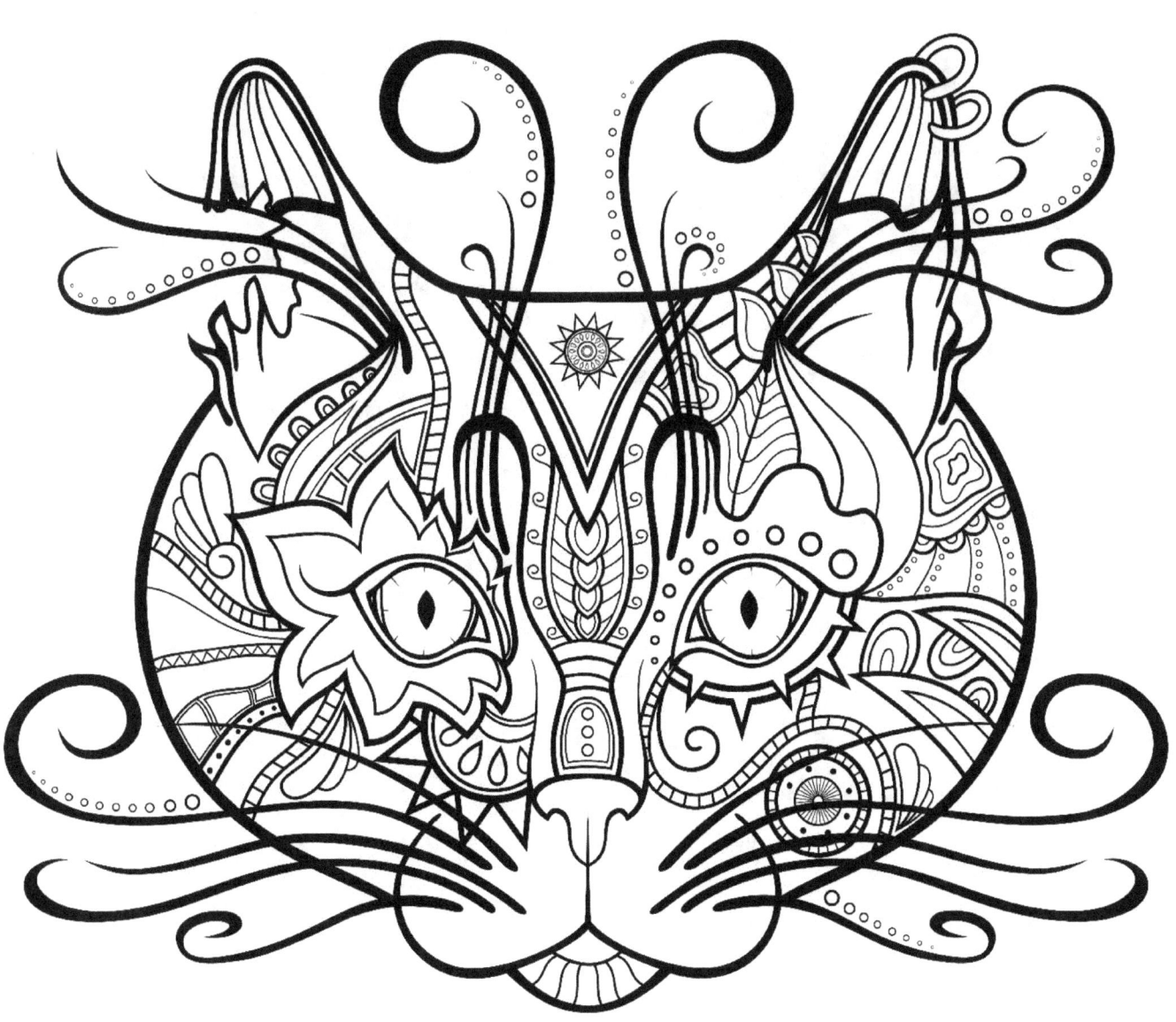

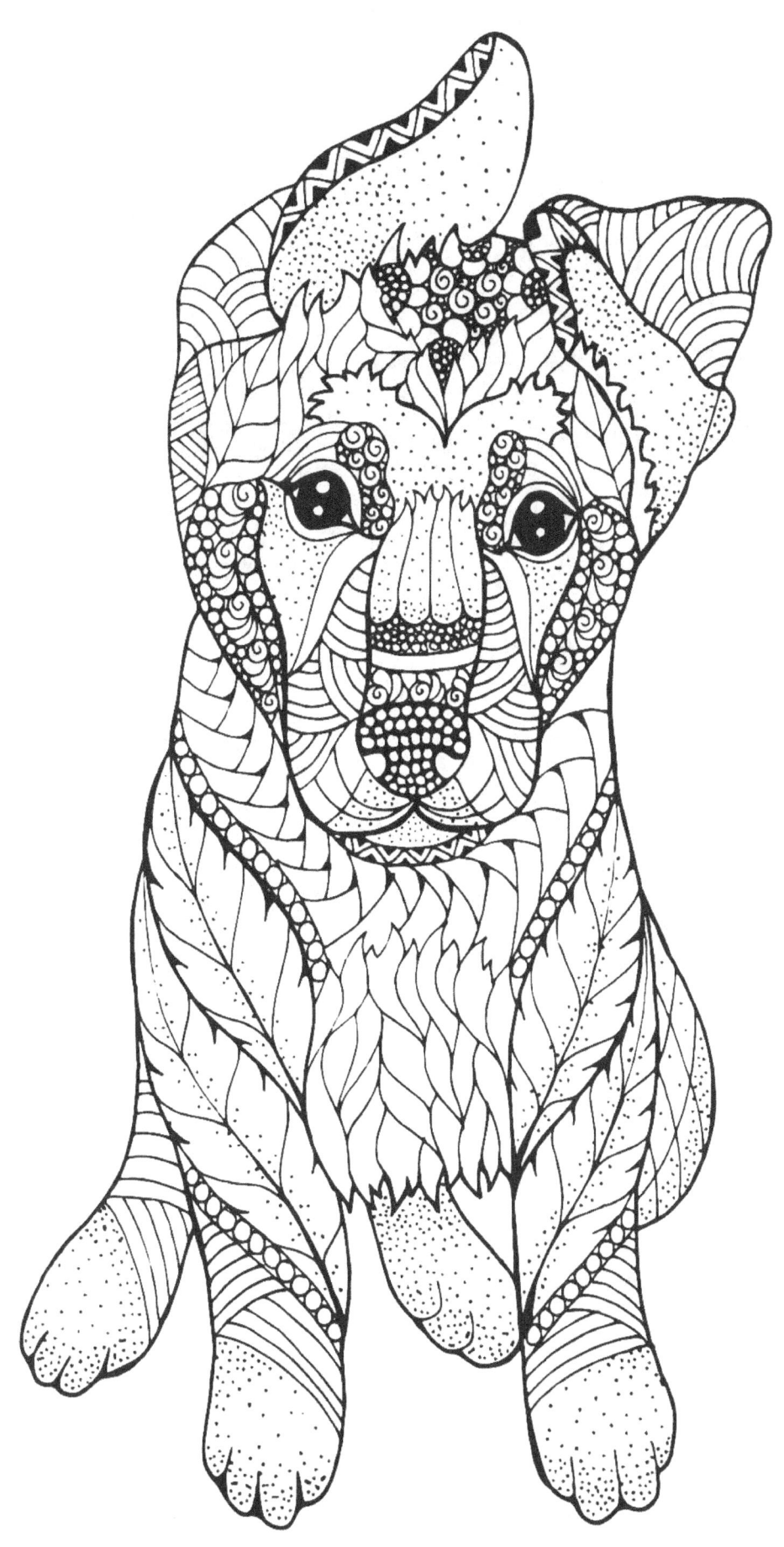

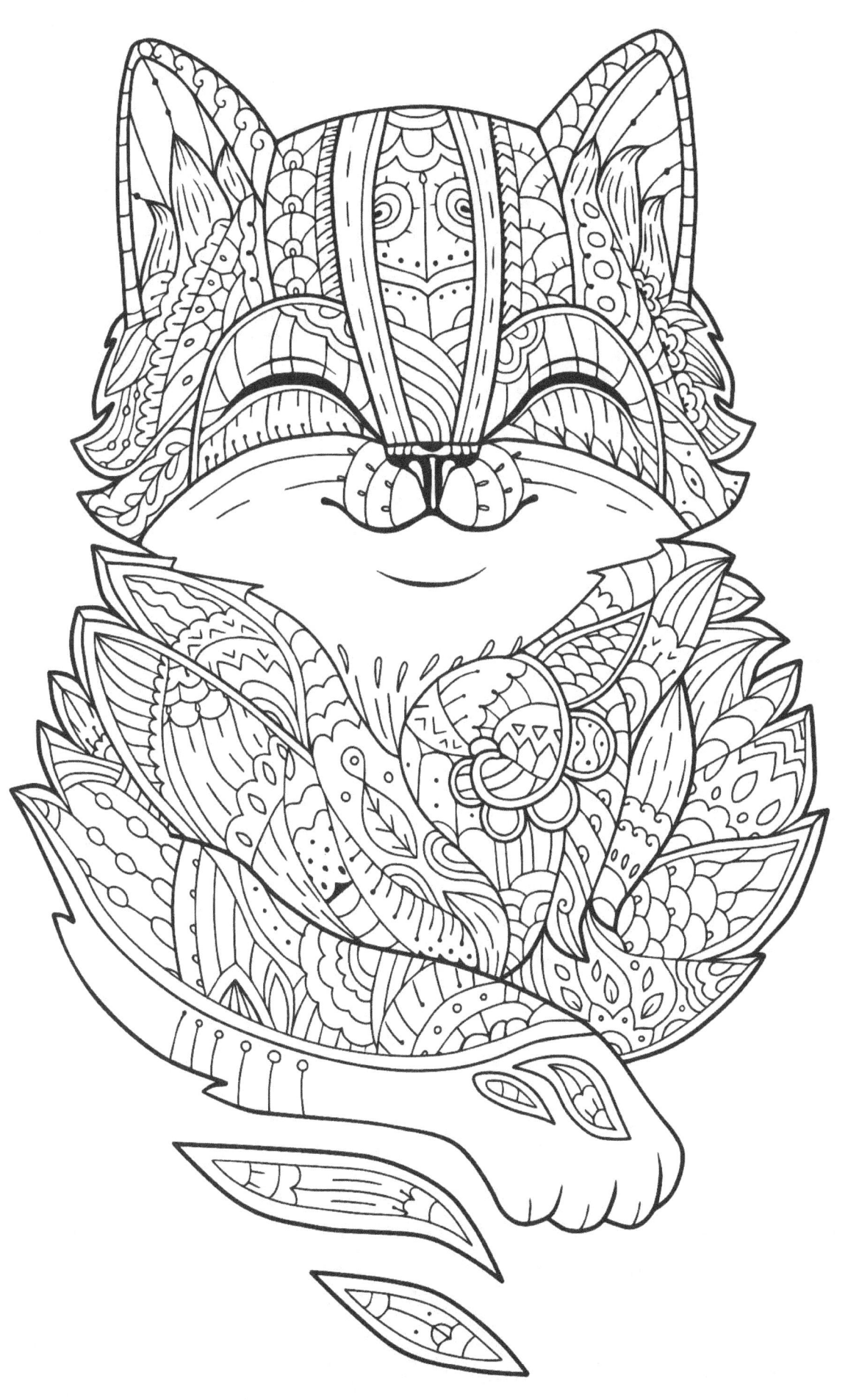

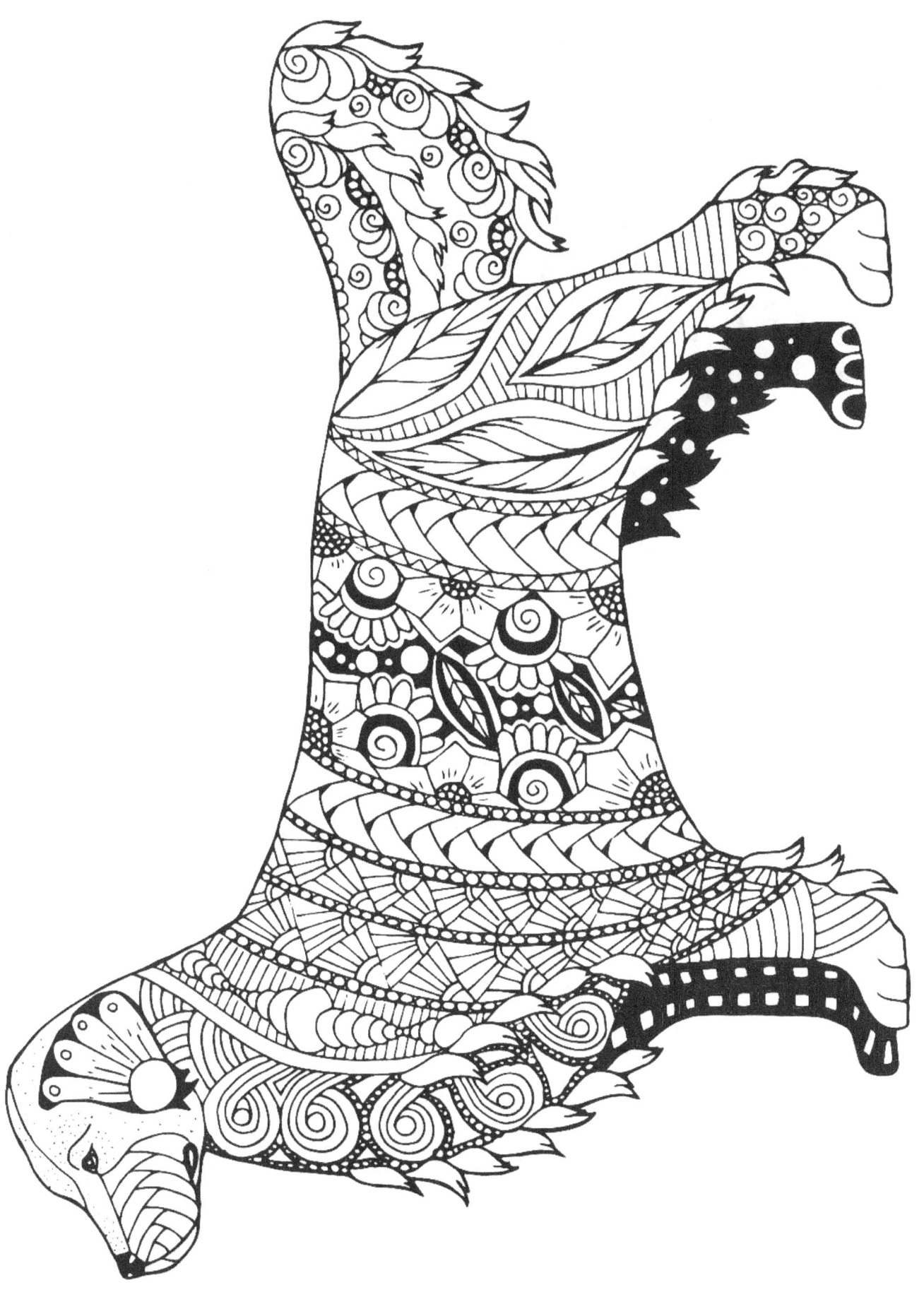

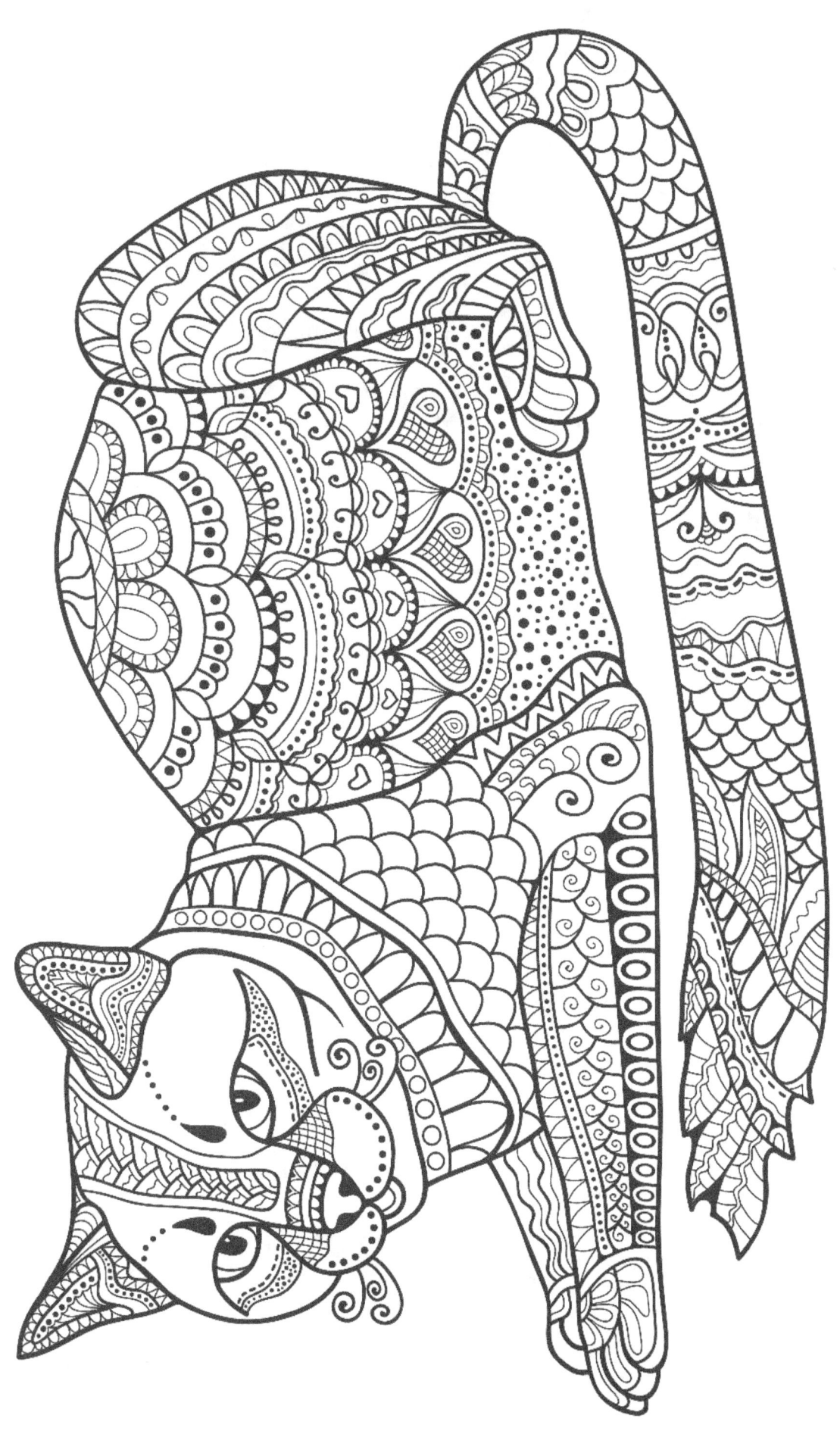

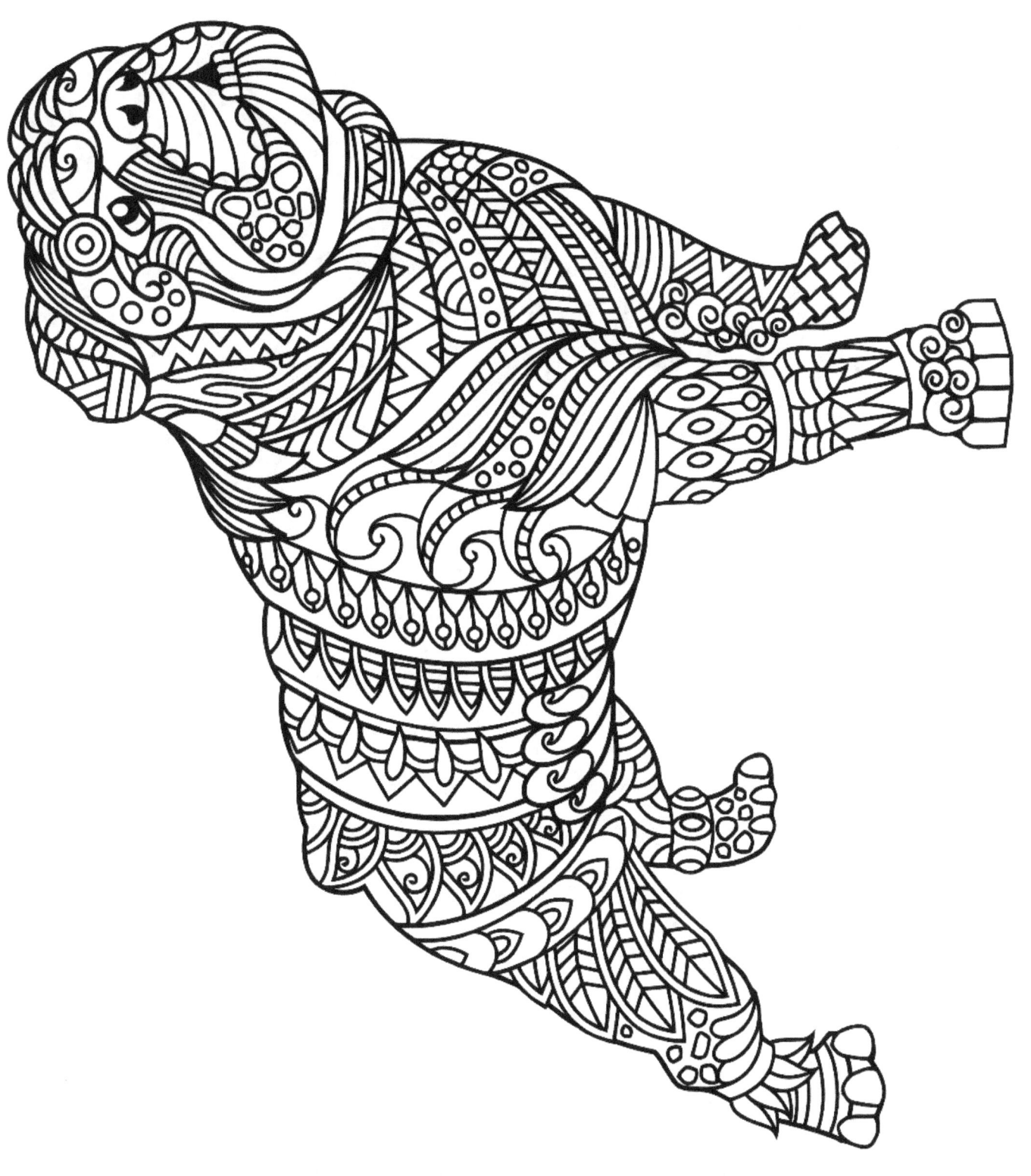

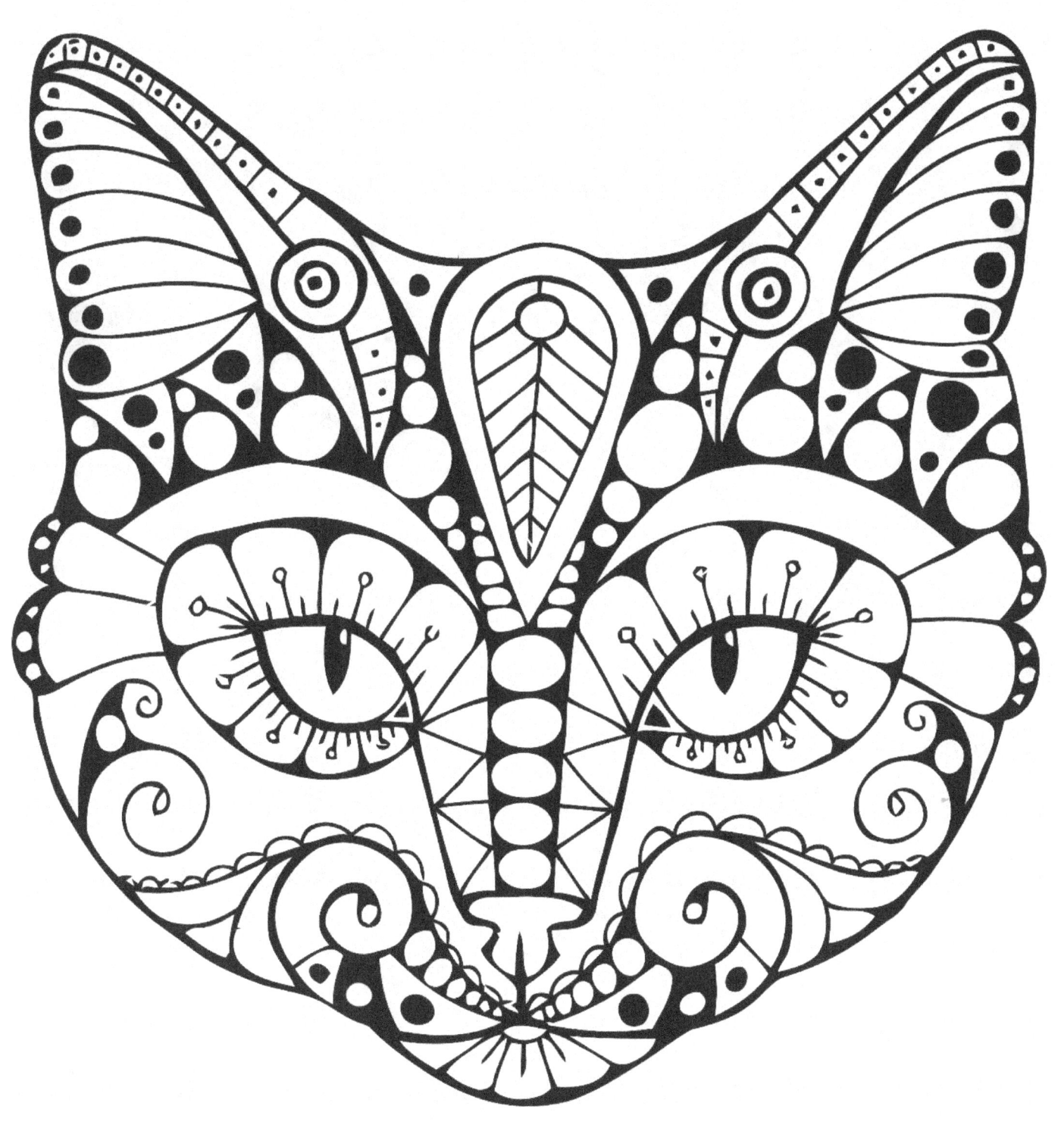

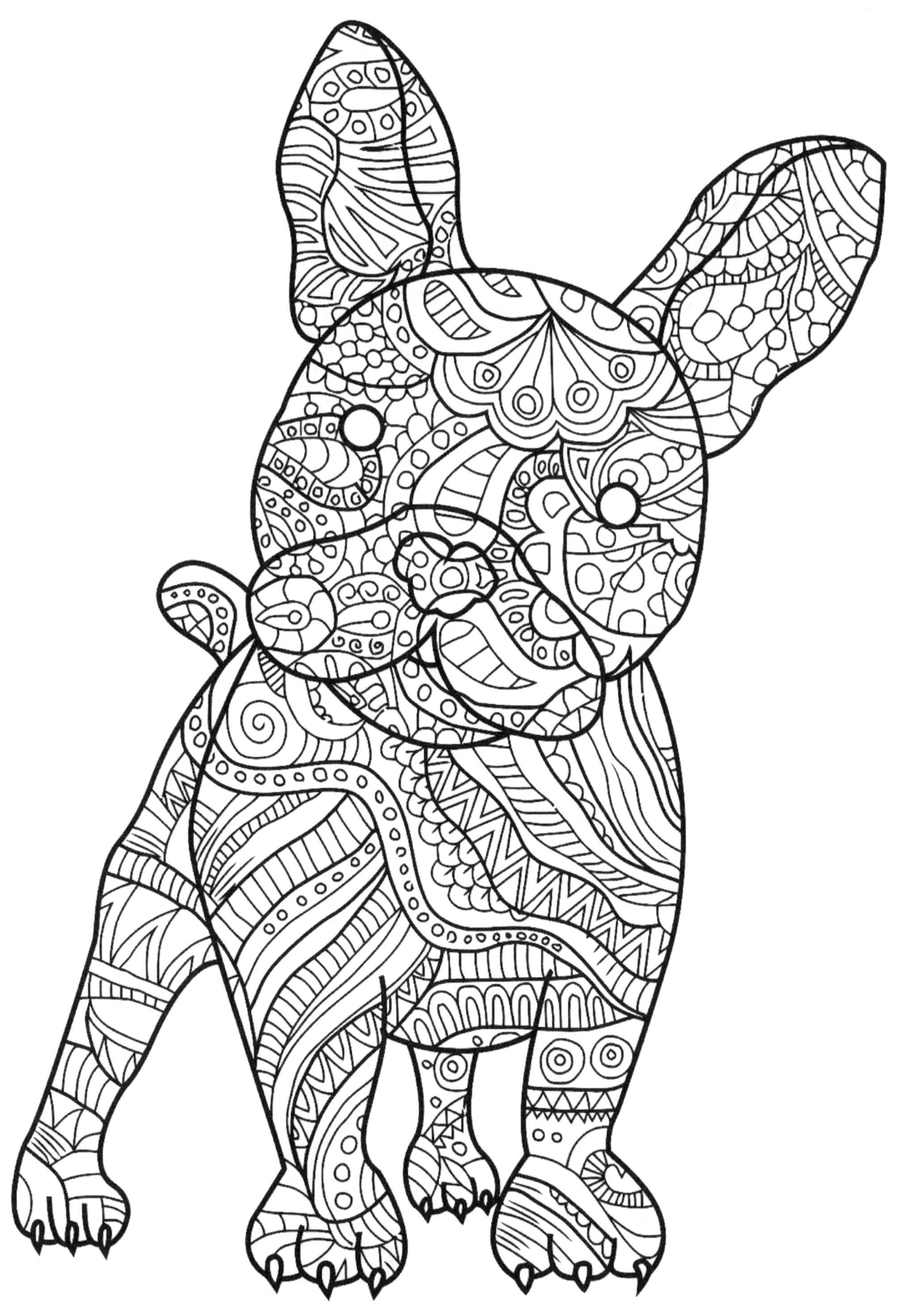

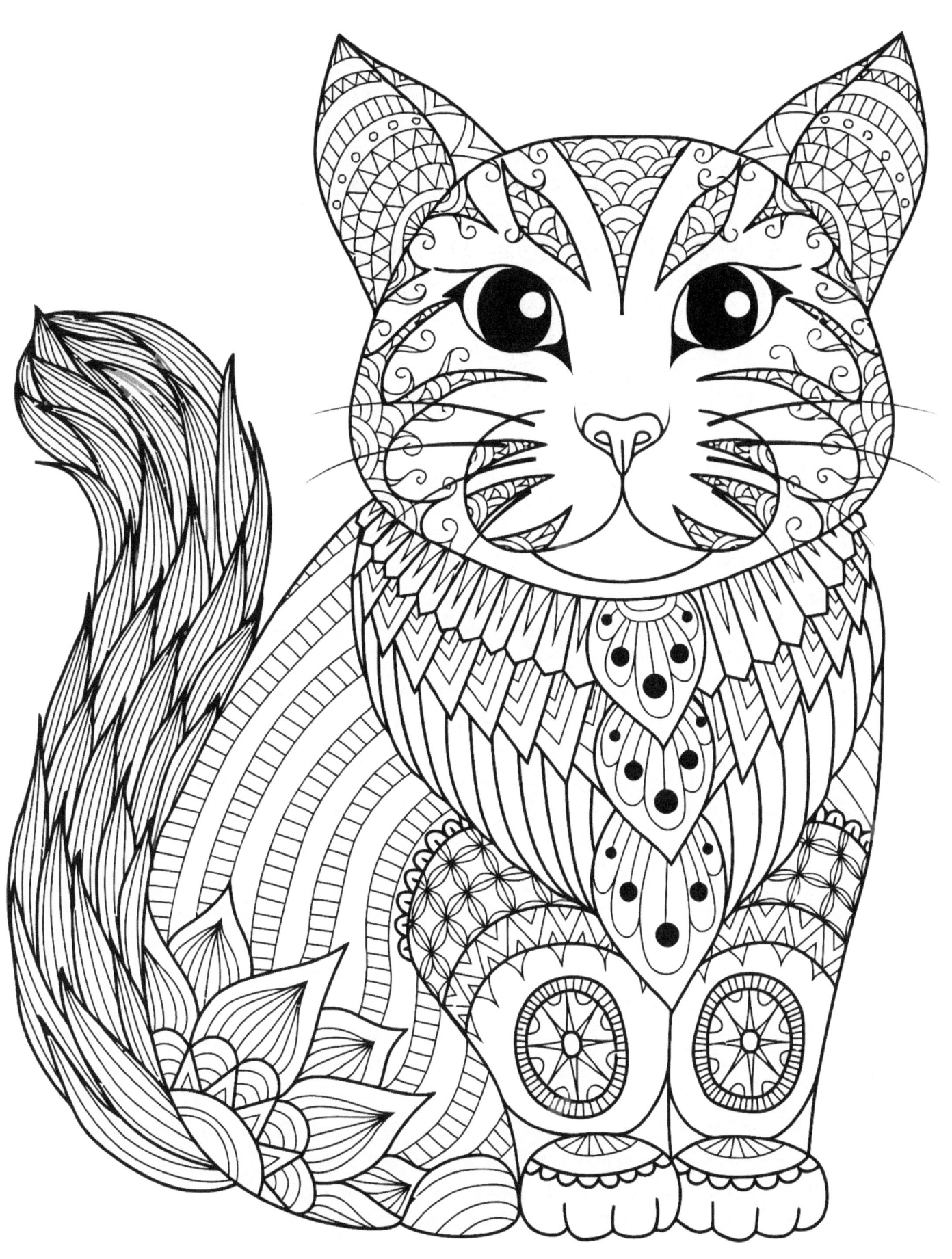

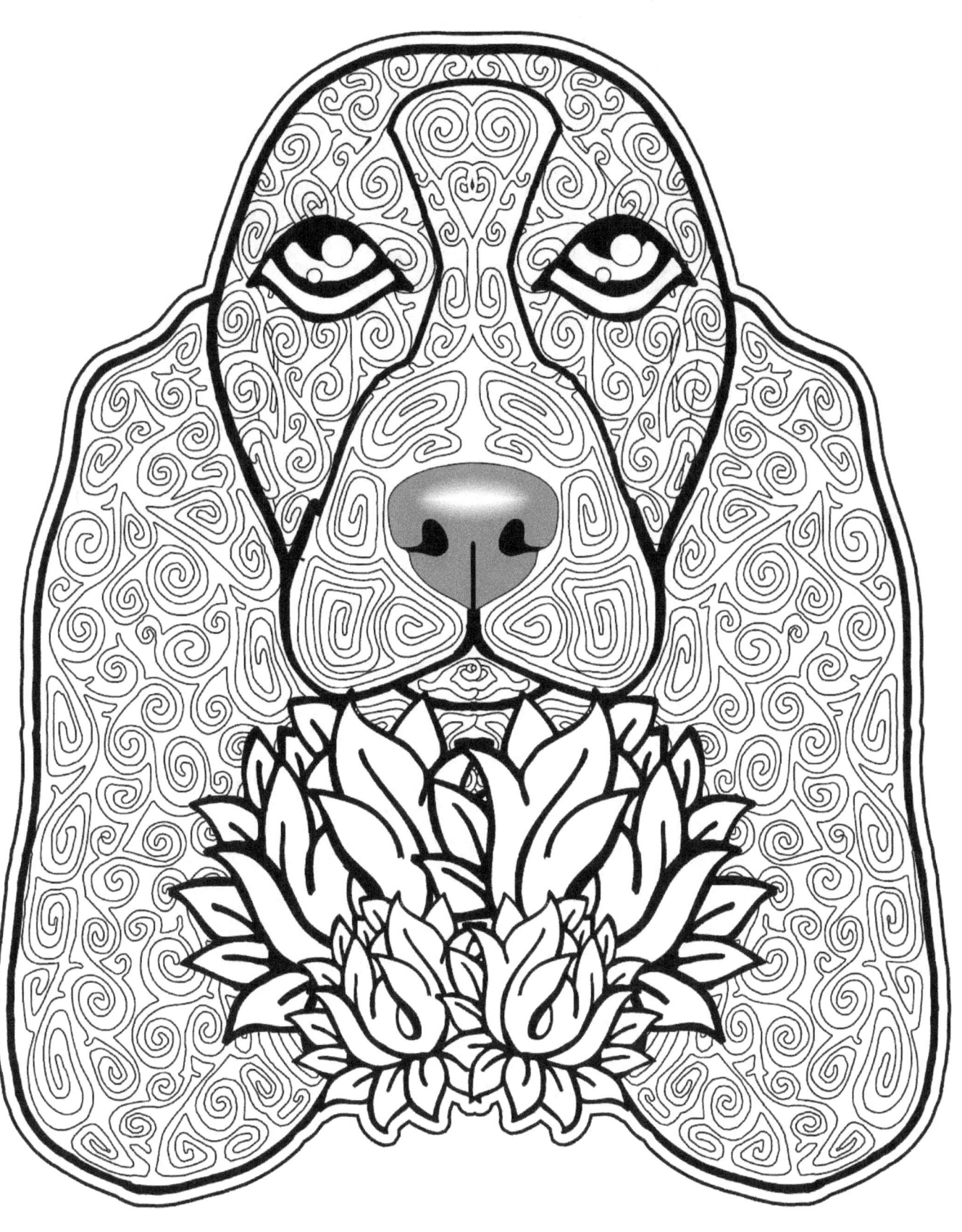

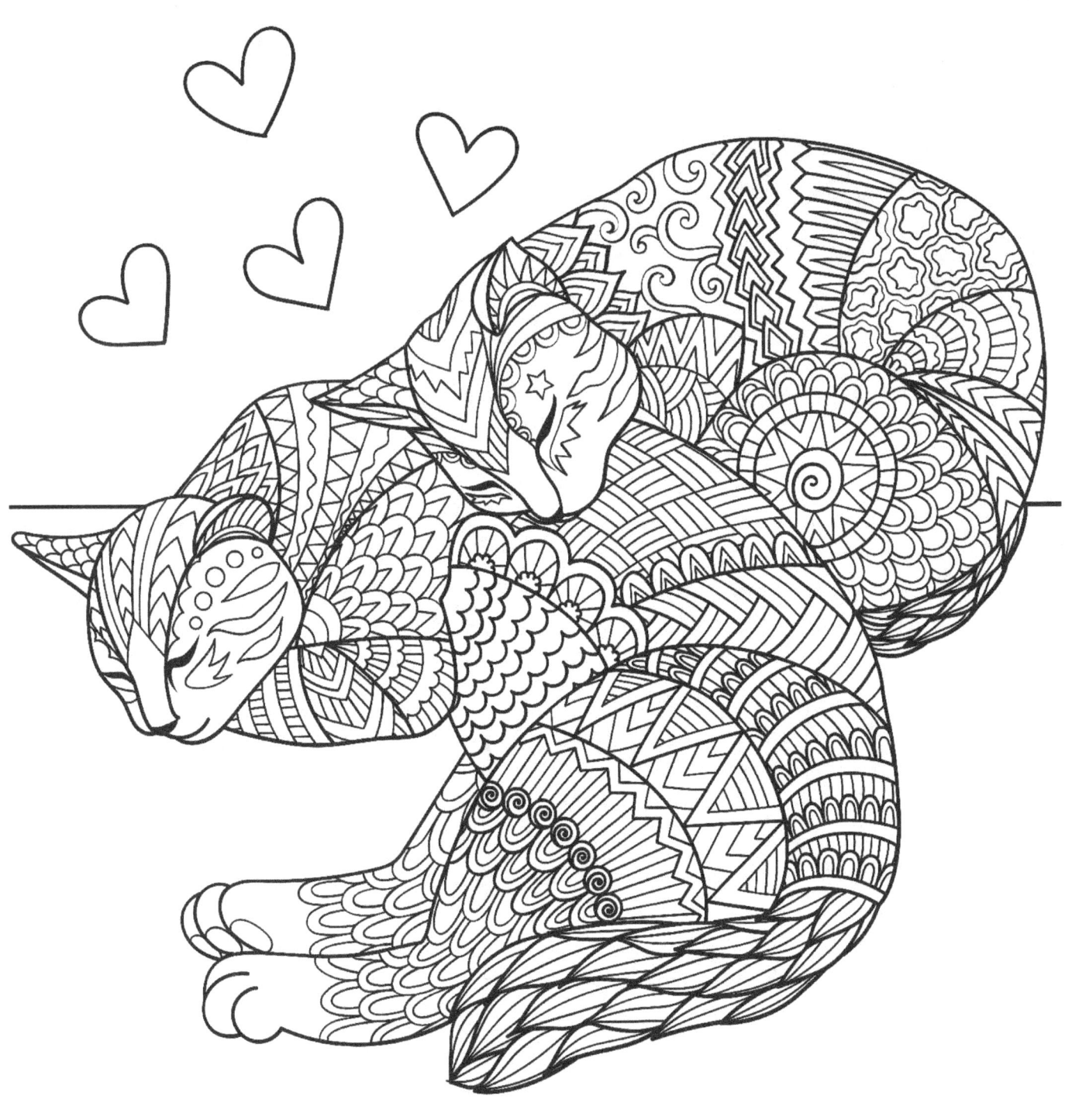

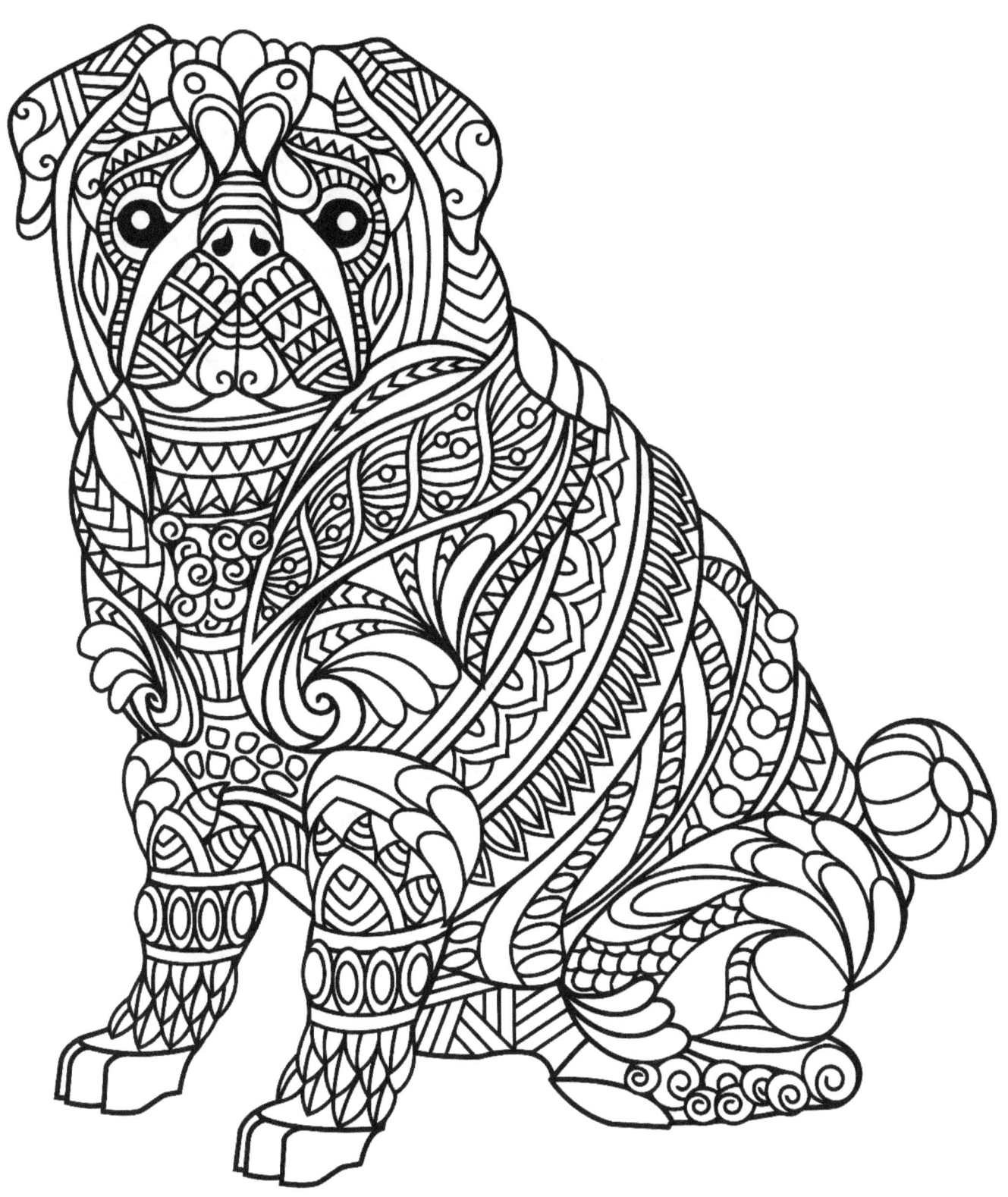

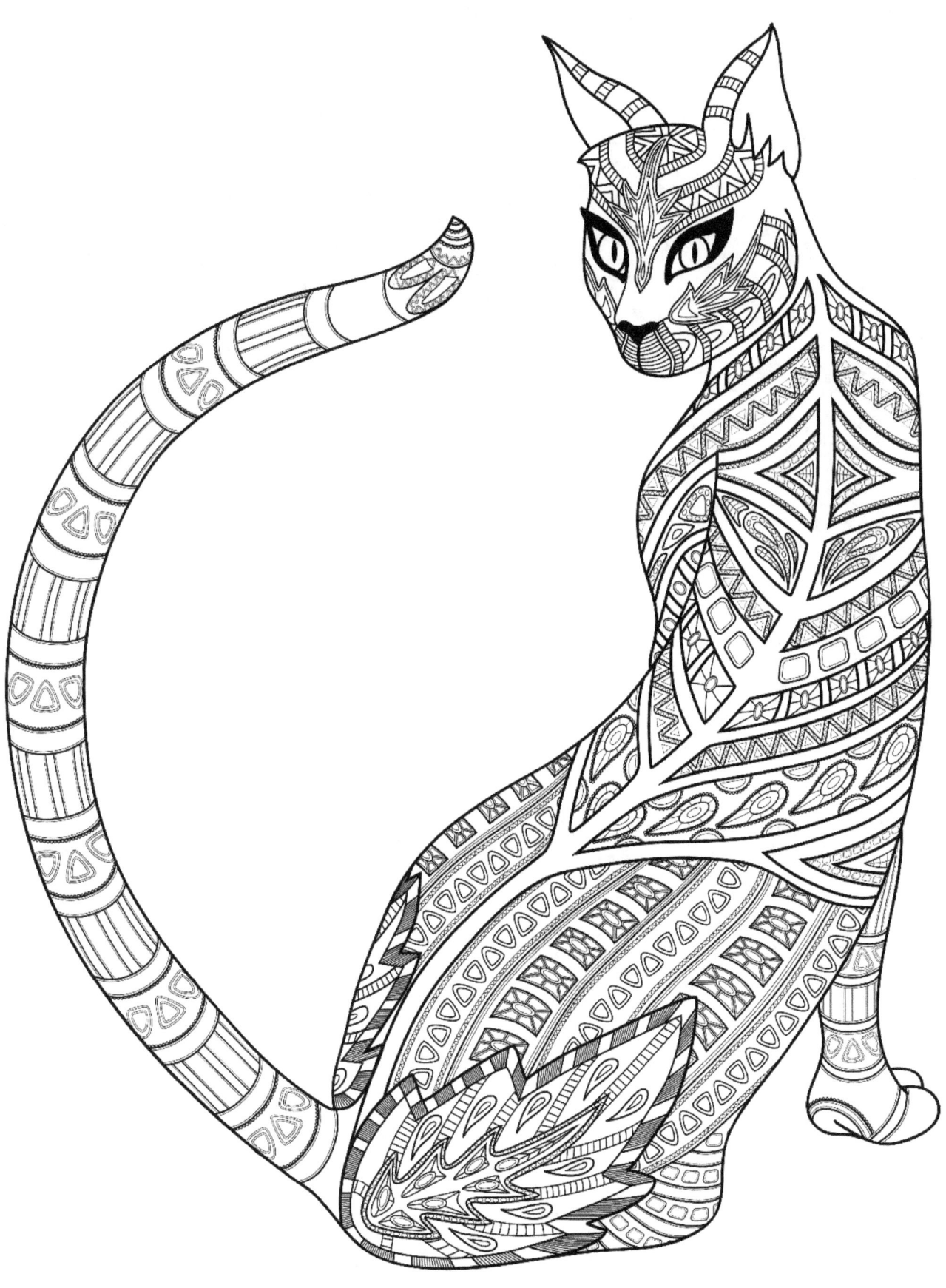

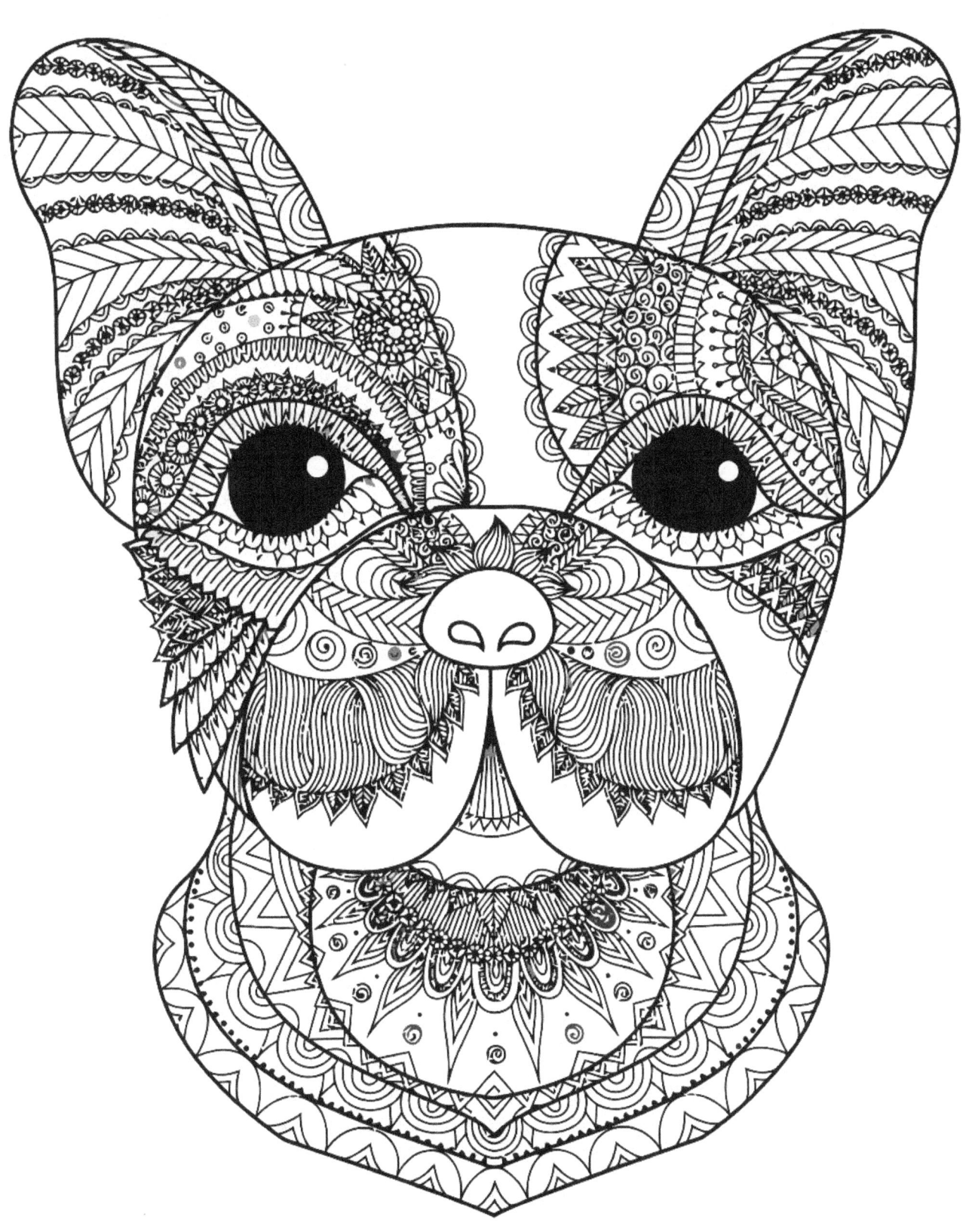

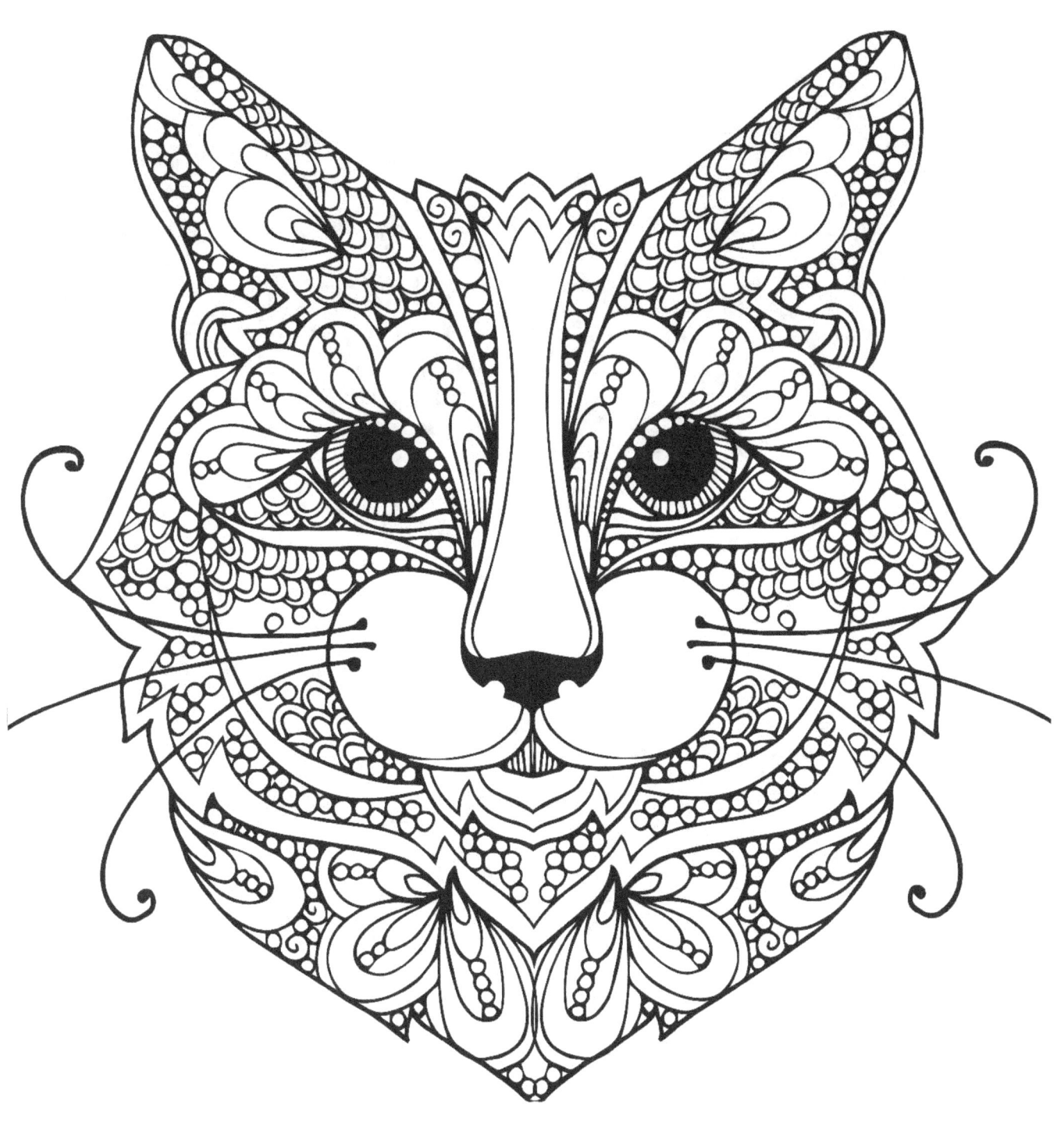

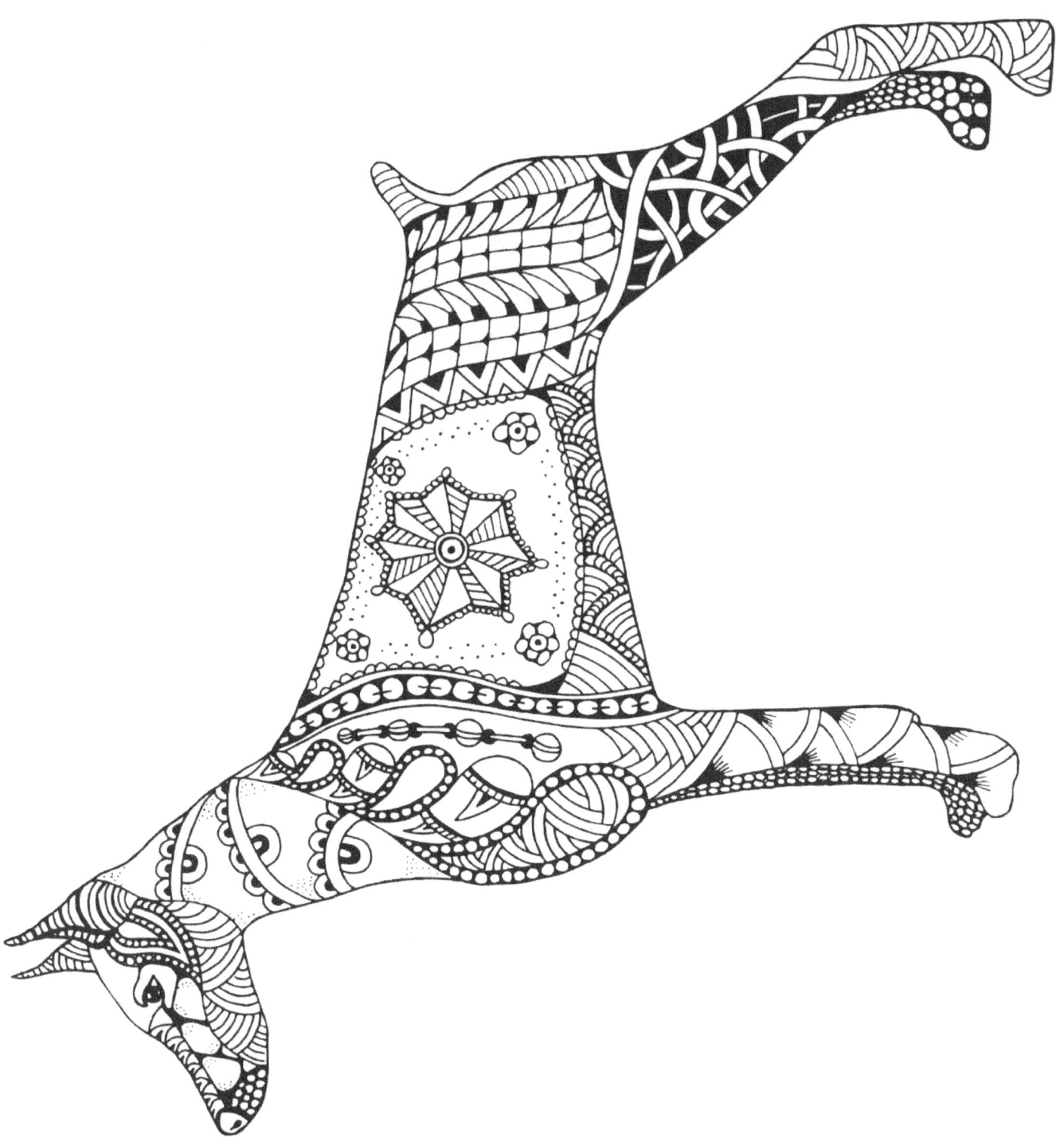

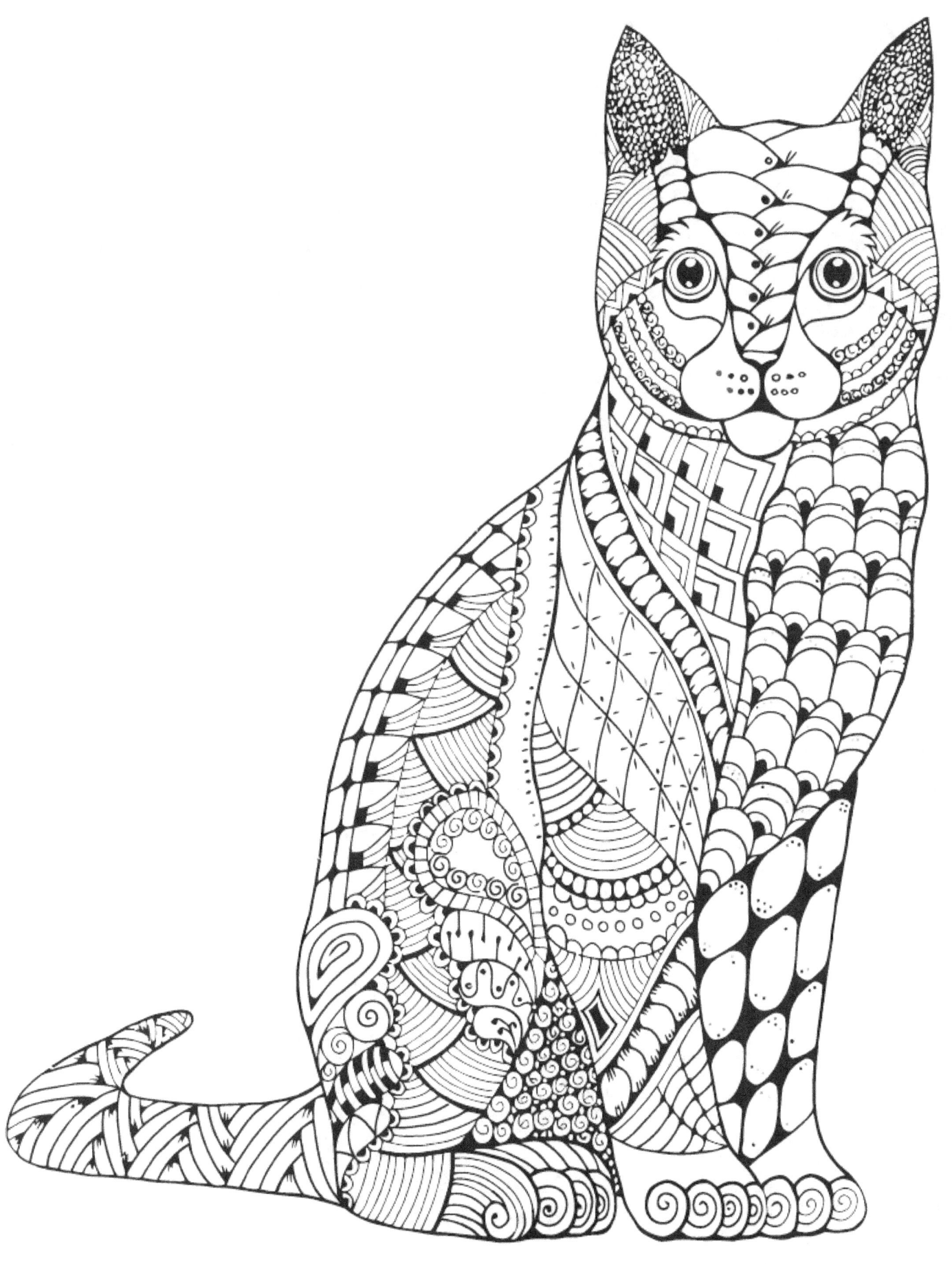

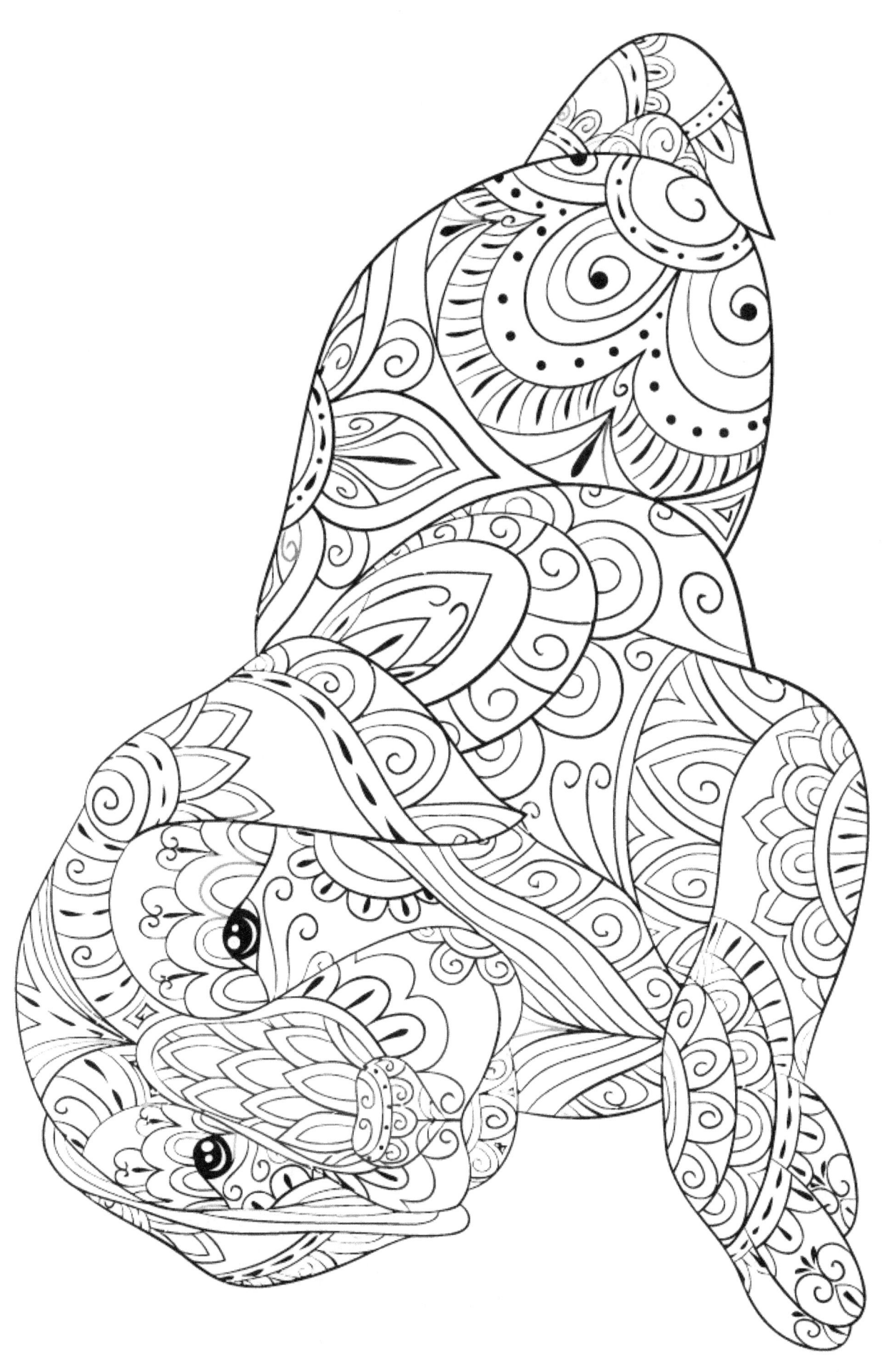

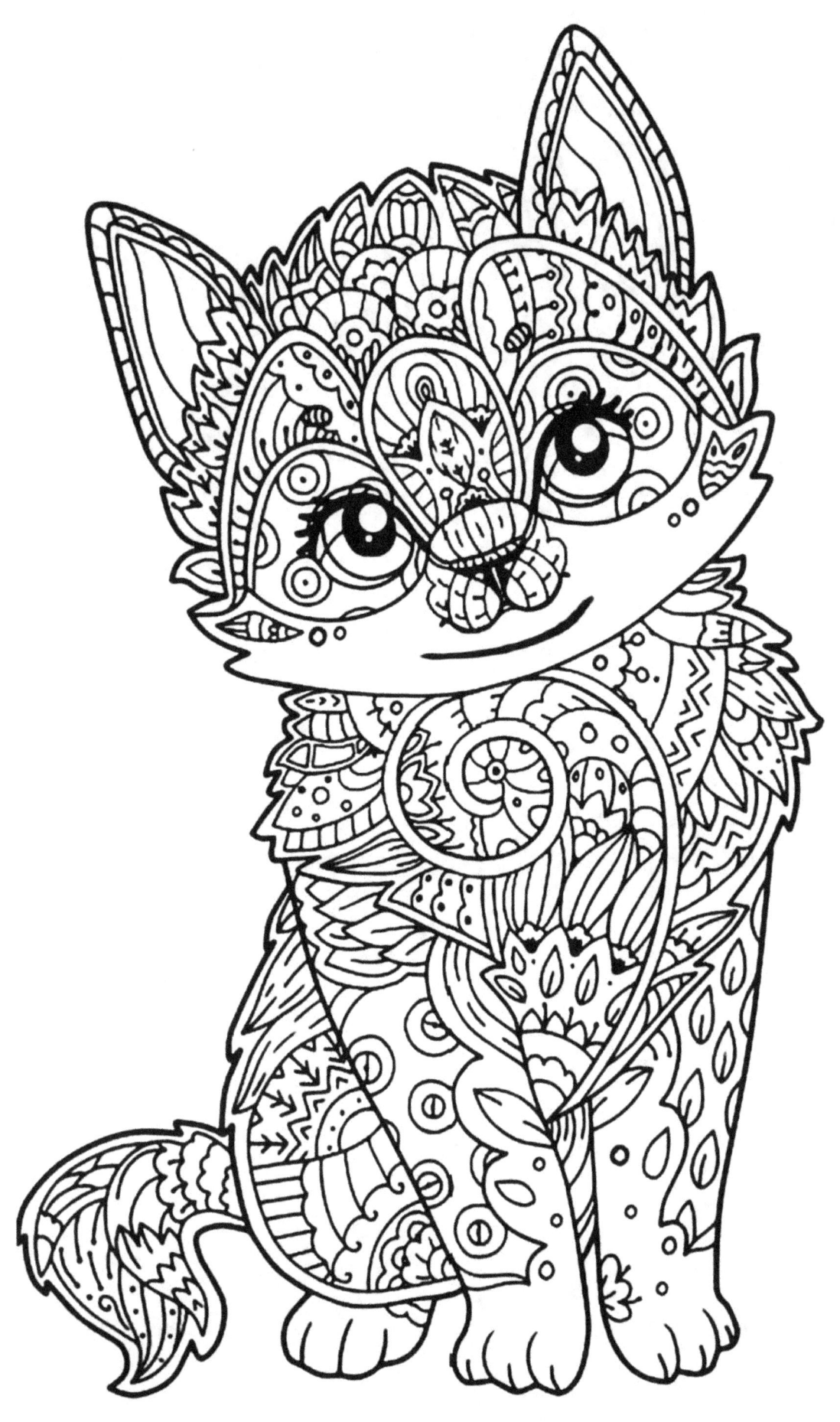

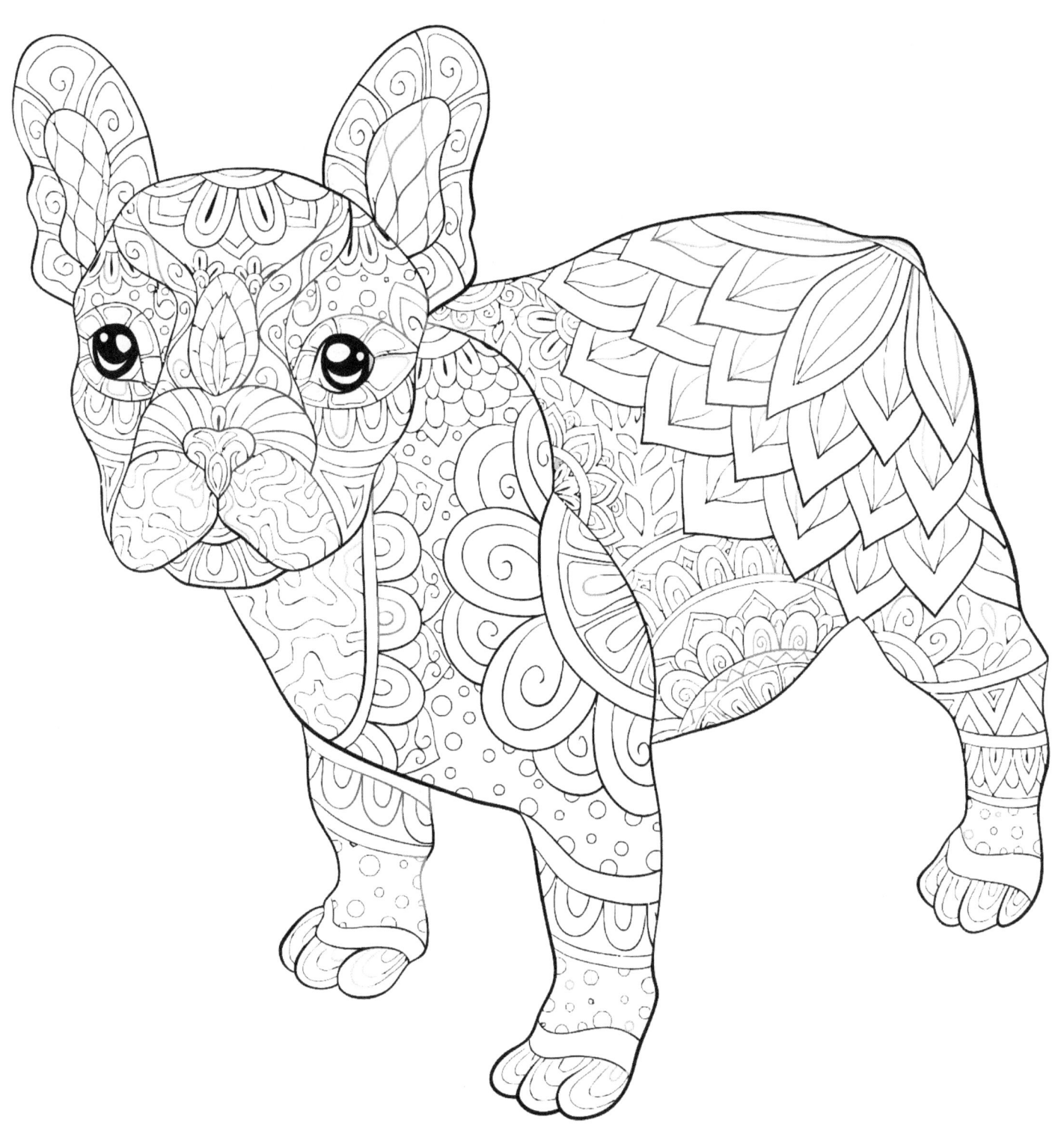

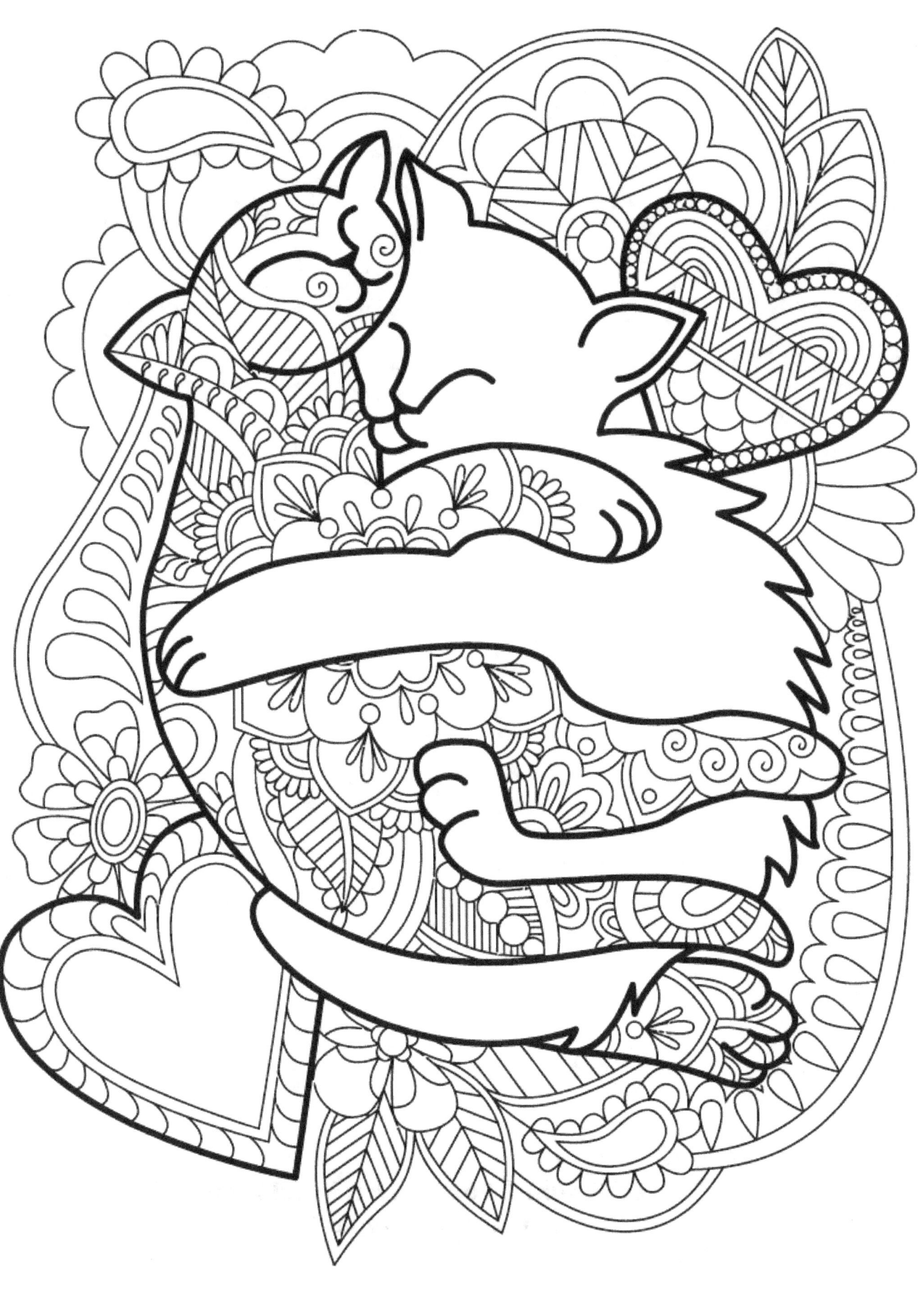

Copyright © 2022 – Wonderful Press
All rights reserved.

www.ingramcontent.com/pod-product-compliance
Lightning Source LLC
Chambersburg PA
CBHW080507220526
45465CB00006B/2402